In Age Rebo~~rn~~
By Grac~~e~~

is a Pa.
offering practical spirituality
to enrich everyday living

"Your word is a lamp to my feet
and a light to my path."
Psalm 119:105

In Age Reborn, By Grace Sustained

One Woman's Journey through
Aging and Chronic Illness

Thelma-Anne McLeod, SSJD

ABC Publishing, Anglican Book Centre
General Synod of the Anglican Church of Canada
80 Hayden Street, Toronto, Ontario, Canada M4Y 3G2
abcpublishing@national.anglican.ca
www.abcpublishing.com www.pathbooks.com

Text set in ITC Legacy Serif and ITC Novarese
Cover and text design by Jane Thornton
Cover photo: Datacraft Co., Ltd/imagenavi/Getty Images

Library and Archives Canada Cataloguing in Publication
McLeod, Thelma-Anne
    In age reborn , by grace sustained : one woman's journey through aging and chronic illness / Thelma-Anne McLeod.

ISBN 978-1-55126-498-1
ISBN 1-55126-498-6

1. McLeod, Thelma-Anne. 2. Parkinson's disease—Patients—Canada—Biography. 3. Chronically ill—Religious life. 4. Chronic diseases—Religious aspects—Christianity. 5. Aging—Religious aspects—Christianity. 6. Faith. I. Title.

RC382.M45 2007   248.8'61   C2007-904059-4

Printed in Canada

Contents

Preface

Writing a personal account of illness as a way to experience spiritual growth and healing is becoming a widespread practice. Such an undertaking not only helps authors to bring their thoughts and experiences into focus; it invites readers, whatever their state of health, to examine their own values and priorities, and perhaps begin a similar journey of discovery.

So it is that I, an Anglican nun in her late seventies with Parkinson's Disease, venture to add yet another book to this growing genre. What can I say that has not been said before? Plenty! Each person is unique, and though there will be similarities among these books, each bears witness to a particular human experience. It has been said that the personal contains and reveals the universal. A book of this kind, then, can bring spiritual growth and renewal to the author by the very process of writing and reflecting deeply on one's experience, and to the reader, who can walk with the writer and find much to share along the way.

Who especially might find insight and clarity by reading such a book? From the responses of those who have read it, I believe *In Age Reborn, By Grace Sustained* will be of interest to a much wider group than people with Parkinson's, their care partners, and family and friends. *In Age Reborn, By Grace Sustained* explores issues that confront everyone. Persons with other chronic progressive illnesses will find commonalities. Those who are experiencing the limitations and changes in status that aging brings will see their experience mirrored in mine. So will those who, whether by aging or life-threatening illness, have come to recognize that the time they have left is brief in comparison with the years already lived, and are having to face up to their own mortality. People in their prime, and indeed individuals of any age who are asking questions about the meaning of life, will find something to ponder. For health professionals, reading this book may help them experience more empathy with patients who are grieving catastrophic events or serious illnesses.

The major issues that I have had to struggle with, and still struggle with, are issues that affect us all:

Communication—being able to articulate what is going on in your body, the need to learn whatever you can about your illness and to share information with family and colleagues;

Maintaining an appropriate independence while recognizing and accepting help that is genuinely needed;

Making the transition from one phase of life to another, particularly from middle age to elderhood and from good health to illness;

Finding creative ways to live with the diminishments that aging and illness bring; coping with the projections and stereotypes of others; recognizing the danger of losing a sense of identity and self-worth, which comes with being on the sidelines; and

Learning how to grieve through your losses to the point that you can be at peace with them.

All these issues are in tension with the values of our society—youth culture, physical fitness, and beauty; personal worth measured by accomplishment, productivity, and conformity to the norms and defining myths of our culture.

This book is written from a Christian perspective, a particular tradition within Christianity, namely the Anglican, and within Anglicanism, an approach that is catholic and at the same time open to reason and experience.

What you are about to read is basically the record of my experience of God's grace in Jesus Christ, of healing where there is no cure. It is also the account of my resistance to grace, the fear of losing myself in answering the call to enter ever more deeply into the way of the cross of Christ. This, too, is an almost universal reaction when people feel that God is getting too close for comfort. Nevertheless, I can truthfully say that during the years since my diagnosis, I have experienced the healing of wounds whose origins are deep in childhood. Grace, as I understand it, is the transforming power of God's love, inviting and enabling us to follow in Christ's footsteps. Whatever your own faith or philosophy, I invite you to walk with me and share in my story—its joys and frustrations, its lessons, its struggles, and above all, its many blessings.

Questions for Reflection and Suggestions for Care

While this book may be read simply for information, or for better understanding of someone you know who has a chronic, progressive illness, *In Age Reborn, By Grace Sustained* also has much to say about how having such an illness affects our spiritual life and practice. To help explore such issues, reflection and discussion questions have been suggested at three levels: for individuals, for care partners and families, and for small groups.

If you have a chronic, progressive illness, working through the questions on your own may help you come to terms with various aspects of your illness. But since Parkinson's (and other such conditions) is a family illness, reading and sharing your experiences, your hopes and fears, may bring a family closer together and improve communication. It may arouse a desire to visit friends and others in your parish or community who have a chronic illness.

The reflection and discussion questions, as well as the "down-to-earth suggestions" at the end of the book, were a collaborative effort, drawing on the professional and intimate experience of several caring and resourceful individuals: Jan Duff, a nurse and clinical scientist involved in Parkinson's research, former Clinical Coordinator of the Parkinson's Clinic in Toronto, and an active volunteer and board member of Parkinson Society Canada; Susan Graham Walker, author of *God, Kids, and Us*, whose experience comes through seven years of service with the ALS Society of Canada and Ontario, and through the neurodegenerative illness of close friends and family; Sandie Jones, coordinator of Client Services Education, Parkinson's Society Canada (central and northern Ontario region); and Suzanne Lawson, a senior executive in the voluntary health sector (ALS, Arthritis, Heart and Stroke) and former care partner to her husband, the late Reverend Art Lawson.

The spiritual journey described in this book is one that most of us take at some time of our life. What I have written about my spiritual journey may well strike a familiar chord in you.

I would be happy to hear from you. My e-mail address is ta@ ssjd.ca and my postal address is St. John's Convent, 233 Cummer Avenue, Toronto, ON M2M 2E8.

Acknowledgements

I wish to express my thanks to the Reverend Mother and Sisters of St. John the Divine for their encouragement and support in enabling me to write this book.

I am especially grateful to those who have undertaken to read and critique the manuscript and offer suggestions and encouragement: Sister Constance Joanna Gefvert, SSJD; M. L. ("Bunny") Stewart, Oblate SSJD; Suzanne Lawson; Jan Duff; Nancy Johnston; Susan Graham Walker; Sandie Jones; Bonnie Black; Anne Tanner; and many others whose encouragement has strengthened my desire to share my story with the much wider readership made possible by publication.

I am grateful to ABC Publishing—to Robert Maclennan, publishing manager, and to my copy editor, Janet Thomas.

Life Before Parkinson's

Since this book deals mainly with the period from autumn 2001 to the end of 2005, four highly significant years of my life, I begin by providing a context, giving a short account of my preceding seventy years. I shall also include some brief notes about Parkinson's, and fuller information about the monastic life, which is perhaps even less known.

I was born in Estevan, Saskatchewan, in 1928, but grew up in Regina. My parents had roots in the Maritime provinces going back to the eighteenth century. Both had long lives. My father (James Archibald McLeod, 1875–1974) was a teacher and later an inspector of schools. My mother (Thelma Audrey Lewis, originally Kinnear, 1894–1990) was a registered nurse. My brother, Henry Wallace McLeod, was a distinguished Spitfire pilot in World War II who was killed in action. My sister, Winnifred Jean McLeod Brunsell, was a primary school teacher. Both siblings having left the nest by the time I was born, I grew up as the only child of parents older than average.

Music has always been an important part of my life. I began piano lessons at age eight, was writing music at twelve, and obtained an associate diploma (ATCM, piano teacher) from the Toronto Conservatory of Music the year I graduated from high school at seventeen. Because I got passing marks in music and straight A's, in school, it never occurred to me to make music a career. I believed that my future lay in the world of scholarship. I went to Queen's University on a provincial scholarship, and graduated in 1950 with a BA honours in English and History, and went on to two well-known American graduate schools, Bryn Mawr College (1950–1951), where I earned a Master's degree, and Radcliffe College (Cambridge, Massachusetts 1951–1952). I never asked myself why I kept on studying; I simply assumed that, since I was an apt student, I would follow an academic career. By the time I reached Radcliffe, however, I began to have serious doubts about my future in the academic world, and did not return after my first year. I went back to my family home in Regina, took a business course (funded by my ever-practical mother), and worked as a stenographer in a law office while waiting to discover what I really wanted to do with my life.

Although I did not recognize it at the time, the answer was implicit in a moment "in time and out of time" given me in 1950, my final year at Queen's. Up to that point I had regarded myself as an agnostic (like my father). While working on an essay on three authors' images of the intersection of time and the timeless, I found myself on my knees, in the unmistakable, self-validating presence of the Divine. This was the major turning point in my life. I had already discovered the Anglican Church and made a mental note that, if I ever came to believe in God, I would become an Anglican. So my immediate response was to be baptized at once (instruction could come later!) and, in due time, confirmed. I began to feel a nudge toward some sort of "church work," but it took several years for me to recognize that I was being called to a monastic community. As time went on, the call became clearer, and finally, on 31 August 1957, I was admitted as a postulant into the Sisterhood of St. John the Divine, an Anglican religious order with its Mother House (main convent and headquarters) in Toronto.

The world of nuns and monks is largely misunderstood in our secular culture. Who in their right mind would give up wealth, independence, and sex for anything as nebulous as a spiritual life? So monks and nuns may be romanticized or portrayed as pathetic or comic relics of the past, out of touch with all that makes life worthwhile. As for Anglicans in religious orders, we often find ourselves having to convince people that we exist! Everyone knows that Henry the Eighth dissolved all the monasteries and convents in England. It is not so well known that, in fact, the "religious life" (in community, under vows) was revived in the Church of England in the mid-nineteenth century and has spread throughout the worldwide Anglican Communion.

The community I belong to was founded in Toronto in 1884. Our ethos is set forth in our Rule of Life:

> We are committed to lifelong conversion and to growth in union with God through the life of prayer and the undivided service of Jesus Christ. In Christ we are both called and sent to be open and responsive to the needs of the church and the world, and to pray and work for peace, justice, unity and the integrity of creation.
>
> —The Rule of Life of the Sisterhood of St. John the Divine (2003)

We strive to lead a balanced life of prayer, service, leisure, and lifelong learning. Besides the convent in Toronto, which is at the heart of our life, we have at present two smaller houses ("branch houses"), one in St-Lambert, Quebec, and the other in Victoria, British Columbia.

We are supported in our vocation by several hundred associates, women and men who commit themselves to prayer and witness to our way of life. Their history goes back to the foundation of our community, when they prayed, worked, and raised funds for the foundation of an Anglican Sisterhood in

Canada. A much more recently formed group are the Oblates, women who because of health, marriage, or age are unable to enter the Sisterhood, but are called to live out its commitment to prayer and service in their own circumstances.

Like any other specialized way of life, the monastic way has a vocabulary of its own. What follows is a description of the process through which one becomes a full-fledged Sister of St. John the Divine. It also provides a glimpse of our day-to-day life.

When a woman comes to *test her vocation*, she spends the first six months as a *postulant* (one who seeks entry). All being well, she receives the *habit* (official garb and symbol of her self-dedication) of the community, thereby becoming a *novice* for three years. She may withdraw from the community or be asked to leave if it becomes clear that her vocation lies elsewhere. At the end of the three-and-a-half-year period, again all being well, she makes the *vows* of poverty, chastity, and obedience for a three-year period (*First Profession*). Finally, she will be elected by her Sisters for *Life Profession*. At that time she will renew her vows and promise to live by them for the rest of her life.

In most Anglican religious orders, the day is structured by worship services at set hours of the day. The *Divine Office* is the name given to this common prayer, which is said or sung in the morning, mid-day (if there is not a service of Holy Communion), late afternoon, and evening. Sisters also commit themselves to two hours of private devotion (*"spiritual duties"*), which includes meditation, pondering the scriptures, and reading that supports our prayer. We pray the Divine Office and attend *Eucharist* (also called the Mass or Holy Communion) together in the chapel and eat together (usually in silence) in the refectory. The Community Room is the place where we have our evening time together in recreation, our house meetings, and our annual general meeting (or *General Chapter*).

In contrast to most Roman Catholic orders, which are either monastic (living a life of prayer, study, work, and leisure within the monastery) or apostolic (engaged in active outside ministry), most Anglican religious orders live the "mixed life," which has both contemplative and active dimensions. Our life is based on the monastic tradition that goes back to St. Benedict (circa 480–547), the father of Western monasticism, with its emphasis on the Divine Office, and a simple and regular life of worship, prayer, study, and leisure. At the same time we have, since our foundation in 1884, been pioneers in education, social work, and hospital administration. We founded the first surgical hospital for women in Toronto and the first convalescent hospital, which now flourishes as St. John's Rehab. At present, hospitality to groups and individuals is an important part of our ministry, and spiritual direction is given by qualified Sisters.

Over the years, I have had a varied ministry, which has used gifts developed before my becoming a postulant and also fostered others latent up to that time. Editorial work, speaking in parishes about our life and work, and later on, leading days of prayer and meditation, retreats, and the occasional parish mission gave scope to my writing abilities and built up my confidence in speaking in public. For a number of years I was responsible for booking speaking engagements, both in-house and at churches, and for assigning Sisters (including myself) to lead such events. This work has taken me from one end of Canada to the other.

My musical training has been well used. I have played the organ from the time I entered the convent up to the present and, almost from the beginning, have written music to be sung in our chapel services. Most of my life in community has been spent at the Mother House; however, I spent five years in our former house in Edmonton and, more recently, four years in our house in St-Lambert, Quebec. I was archivist at the Mother House for a few years, and served as assistant to the Reverend Mother from 1996 to 1999 when, for reasons of health, I asked to be relieved.

In addition, I have served on several committees of the Anglican Church at both national and diocesan levels. Most memorable for me were my eleven years with the task force that produced *Common Praise*, the current hymn book of the Anglican Church in Canada. This task drew upon my experience in revising hymn texts, making them gender inclusive while maintaining their stylistic qualities and excellence. Paul Gibson, at that time the liturgical officer of the Anglican Church of Canada, and I were responsible for the reworking of a good many hymns, besides the texts I had already revised for use in our convent.

Although I will provide detailed information about Parkinson's Disease (PD) in the context of my story, I would first like to share some basic facts about this disease. PD is one of the most common neurological disorders and is predicted to double in incidence in the next ten years, yet most people know little about it. The four basic symptoms of the disease are a resting tremor, muscular rigidity, slowness of movement, and balance problems. Many other symptoms, such as changes in sleep pattern, shuffling gait, and diminished arm swing when walking, soft speaking voice, fatigue, depression, a mask-like face, and small, cramped handwriting, to name a few, may also be present. Parkinson's is a highly individualized condition. Given that in a group of people with Parkinson's you may find one or two who have the same symptoms as yourself, it is not surprising that "symptom swapping" is a popular indoor sport!

While no cure exists at the present time, much research is going on, and researchers are optimistic about finding a cure within ten to fifteen years. Meanwhile, medications can control symptoms effectively during the first several years of PD. After that, side-effects are likely to occur. Nevertheless, it is not unusual for people with PD to lead productive lives for many years.

The Stranger
Who Came to Stay

Lord, you have searched me out and known me....
You trace my journeys and my resting-places....
For you yourself created my inmost parts;
you knit me together in my mother's womb.
I will thank you because I am marvellously made;
your works are wonderful, and I know it well....
How deep I find your thoughts, O God!
how great is the sum of them!
(Psalm 139, selected verses, *The Book of Alternative Services*)

I do not know when the journey began. I have read that, long before symptoms appeared, cells were quietly self-destructing deep within my brain. I have read, too, that the anxiety and depression that beset me during the decade before my diagnosis could have resulted from chemical changes in the brain associated with that cell death.

Although I had been ailing for a few years, I did not know it. As early as 1996, in Edmonton, I was falling for no apparent reason. There were some spectacular falls, like toppling off a stile between two fields; embarrassing falls, like tripping over my bedspread and bruising my arm on the way to the floor; and routine falls during walks, caused by what I scarcely noticed at the time, a dragging right foot. A weakness in my right leg prevented me from raising it high enough to put my foot into a pant-leg. My right eyelid developed a droop. In the light of what I know now, I can recognize these silent precursors. At the time, even as the signs became more obvious, I remained unsuspecting. Since I had enjoyed robust health for seventy years, it never occurred to me that I might develop a chronic illness.

It was in February 1999 that the superstructure of my life began to totter when, as assistant to the Reverend Mother, a position that I had found so fulfilling and exhilarating, I suddenly collapsed under a burden of anxiety, dread, physical deterioration, and general immobility. I thought it was burn-out. Rest and less demanding responsibilities would set things right.

Things did improve, and when I transferred from the Mother House in Toronto to our community's branch house in St-Lambert, Quebec, in the spring of 2000, the excitement and challenge of a new assignment and a new milieu buoyed me up. When winter came, however, I began to notice changes. I moved more slowly. I was getting very stiff (the effect of the Montreal winter, no doubt, on a recently arrived Torontonian). Sometimes I had to pull myself out of my refectory chair by grabbing hold of the table. When out on my daily exercise walk, I found myself short of breath or inexplicably slowing down, and my arms hung at my sides. For no apparent reason, my handwriting was becoming small. As well, my mental processes were changing. It took me longer to process information. I often did not take in what was being said. I found it hard to concentrate, and when I spoke, I seemed unable to get across what I wanted to say.

At 72, surely I was too young to be showing such physical and mental signs of old age. Yet I was acting old, and worse still, I was being perceived as being old. I could not keep up with the pace of life, and this brought its own pain. But spring would come, I told myself, and things would improve.

Spring came, and summer. At the cottage, I took on an energetic program of exercise walking. I began to work with weights. Surely this would reverse the trend. It was not to be. When I returned to the Mother House for General Chapter, 2001, it was apparent to others, though not yet to myself, that all was not well. My gait was slow and shuffling. My arms were rigid. My right leg was developing a noticeable tremor. My speech was hesitant. I lacked my former sparkle. "What's wrong with Thelma-Anne?" Sisters were asking.

When I had an interview with Sister Constance Joanna (my friend, as well as my Reverend Mother), she told me that the Sisters in my house were concerned about me. When she mentioned that they had been looking up web sites on Parkinson's Disease, I exploded. What right had they to play at amateur diagnosis? (Later I learned that Sister Elizabeth, whose mother had Parkinson's, had observed enough similarities in me to make her suspicious.) At any rate, I was due for my annual physical check-up when I got back to St-Lambert. I agreed that I would discuss my symptoms with my physician.

Rereading the notes from my annual eight-day retreat at Loyola House, Guelph, Ontario (2001), I can see how I was being prepared spiritually for what lay ahead. When I came into retreat, I was just emerging from a period in which prayer was a dull routine, yielding neither comfort nor challenge. God seemed remote, and scriptures, even my favourites, left me cold. Yet even in what seemed like total desolation, words or images came into the void from time to time—just enough to keep me from despair and to let me know that growth was happening.

In retreat, much healing took place. Emotionally, it was as if a deep-seated abscess began to drain and healthy, new tissue to form. Long-standing shame, fear, and resentment, parental expectations that had dominated my life, a sense of worthlessness and inadequacy, all came to the surface to be seen for what they were, and to receive God's healing touch.

I realized that finding God was not a matter of being freed from pain, but of sharing God's pain; that God made me to be exactly who I am, in order to share in God's redemptive work. If I were perfectly well adjusted and happy, I might well be impervious to others' pain, totally self-centred and self-absorbed. I learned that gifts must be both received and accepted; that we not only use, but are used by, that with which we are gifted.

After retreat, one usually comes down from the mount of vision into the grubby realities of daily life and the tangled skein of human relationships. Grand visions are not easily translated into action. And so it was for me. But looking back, I can see that some important issues had been raised and needed to remain current if I was to meet the challenge that lay ahead.

I came to my medical appointment armed with a long list of symptoms. Before I had got halfway through, my doctor started asking me questions. "Was my handwriting getting smaller?" (Yes, the Sisters had been after me to write larger, but how could *she* know?) She spoke words that brought clarity and comfort: "You have the beginnings of Parkinson's. *We can help you.*" I left the doctor's office with a referral to a neurologist, relieved to know that I had something identifiable and treatable, and doubly relieved to know that it wasn't Alzheimer's.

Before I could make the appointment, I had to go to Edmonton to help the Sisters with the work of closing down our sixty-five-year-old St. John's Priory. In conversation with one of our volunteers, I learned that her husband had been coping with Parkinson's for seventeen years. We agreed that he should come and talk with me. He drove himself over one day, and we had a good conversation. He spoke of his own experience, and of what I might encounter as the condition progressed.

He also left me a number of pamphlets and brochures, including *Taking Charge: A Guide to Living with Parkinson's* (Susan Calne, *et al.*, Parkinson Society Canada, 1999). As I read, I found descriptions of a wide range of symptoms that I recognized at once, but had never thought of as having a common cause. I learned that depression and anxiety can be present for years before the more recognizable symptoms appear. I learned that it was quite typical for emotions to lie near the surface, and that the slightest thing, happy or sad, can reduce one to tears. I learned that there are more graceful ways of getting out of a chair than the way I had devised. In a word, I read much that could have been written about me, and for me.

When I returned to St-Lambert, I too was looking up web sites, determined to learn all I could about the condition with which I would be living for the rest of my days. I discovered that Parkinson's Disease (named after James Parkinson, the nineteenth-century English physician who was the first to describe it) is "a progressive neurodegenerative disease that mainly affects movement.... Nerve cells in the brain communicate by using chemicals called neurotransmitters. The neurotransmitter involved in movement is called dopamine. When the cells that produce it die, they can no longer send signals for movement. By the time Parkinson's Disease has been diagnosed, approximately 80 per cent of dopamine-producing cells have already stopped functioning" (*A Manual for People Living with Parkinson's Disease*, Parkinson Society Canada, revised 2003). I vaguely remembered having heard of dopamine, but I had no inkling of how vital it is to so many functions I had taken for granted, and what can happen when it is in short supply.

The major symptoms are tremor, slowness and stiffness of movement, impaired balance, and rigidity of muscles. In addition, there is a host of other symptoms, some of which I recognized as my own. I was learning a whole new vocabulary. Some of the symptoms to which these terms applied I had already experienced:

bradykinesia (the slowness of movement typical of Parkinson's); and *micrographia* (smallness of handwriting, often an early symptom);

Others lay ahead:

Resting tremor—In Parkinson's, I learned, the tremor is experienced when the body part is not moving and disappears when movement begins. Most people associate Parkinson's with tremors, but in fact, some 20 to 30 per cent of people with Parkinson's never develop them. Since mine appeared rather late, people kept saying, "You don't *look* as if you have Parkinson's!"

Festination—a kind of rapid walking with tiny steps and the body leaning forward. This is associated with balance problems and often leads to falls.

Dyskinesia—involuntary movements of various parts of the body, wiggling movements, sometimes vigorous and at other times smoother, and not like tremor. The movements do not usually appear until the body has been exposed, or sensitized, to medications that contain levodopa, intended to replace the dopamine that the brain cannot supply adequately or to mimic its action ("dopamine agonists"). These movements are a side-effect of treatment rather than a symptom of the disease.

Soon after my return from Edmonton, I made an appointment with the neurologist to whom I had been referred. On 11 October 2001, I arrived at her office. I was somewhat awed by this tall, elegant woman who proceeded to examine me in a very business-like way. "You have Parkinson's. It needs to be treated." When I asked about how the condition might progress, she exclaimed, "Seventy-three! You will have twenty good years and die of something else." She gave me some medication and told me to return in two weeks.

Standard treatment for the symptoms of Parkinson's is to replace some of the dopamine that the brain can no longer produce. Since the dopamine molecule is too large to cross the blood-brain barrier, a substance called levodopa is prescribed. When levodopa enters the brain, it is metabolized into dopamine. This treatment produces side-effects in the course of time, so other medications are often prescribed. I discovered that the medication I was given, Requip, was a dopamine agonist.

The e-mail I sent to the houses of our community after my appointment with the neurologist reflected the buoyancy and relief I felt:

I am feeling optimistic, and thankful that I have started a course of treatment that promises substantial improvement. Right now, a lot of my energy goes into living with symptoms, especially the chronic tiredness and mood fluctuations. It will take a few weeks for the medication to kick in, but when it does, I'll begin to feel and act more like my old self. Meanwhile, I know I can count on your prayers.

On my second appointment, the neurologist had me walk across the waiting room. "That medication isn't doing you any good," she declared. "Throw it in the garbage." She then wrote a prescription for Sinemet CR 100/25 (synthetic dopamine), one tablet to be taken a half-hour before rising and another in the early afternoon, and sent me on my way.

On the very first morning, I noticed a difference. A day or so later, on an outing in the Eastern Townships, I sprinted up a small hill. "Did you see that?" I exclaimed in delight. "Just call me Dopamine Daisy!" A few days later, when we went to the convent in Toronto for the Life Profession of our Sister Anne, the improvement was evident to all.

At the same time, I felt frustrated. My Sisters were supportive, but I felt I could not really communicate with them because I lacked the words and concepts to explain what I was experiencing. One day in mid-November, I decided to act. I telephoned the Parkinson Society Québec for information. Later that week, I presented myself at their office, announced that I wanted to become a member, and paid my dues. I spent the rest of the morning in their library, and borrowed a book, *Caring for the Parkinson Patient* (J. Thomas Hutton and Raye Lynne Dippel, eds., 1999), which provided fascinating reading for weeks afterward.

Having packed a lunch, I shared noon-hour conversation with Annie Lavigne, the Montreal regional coordinator. I asked if there was a support group on the South Shore. Yes, there was, but it was in French. The possibility of forming an English-speaking group caught my imagination. "Count me in!" I exclaimed, and went on to suggest that we might have suitable space at St. John's House.

So the "stranger" whom I had housed unwittingly for possibly a decade made its presence known, and served notice that it was going to share my house as long as I inhabited it. Its presence would make significant changes in my life, both in terms of having to adapt myself to limitations, and in the potential it offered for the healing of dysfunctional habits and attitudes that, unknown to me, had worked against my happiness and peace of mind and prevented me from giving myself generously to others.

Best of all, the "stranger" would bring me to a greater awareness of God's unconditional love, as I struggled not only with the heritage of my past, but also with the turmoil of the present and, given the progression of my illness, the uncertainty of the future.

Suggestions for Reflection/Discussion

For Individuals
- Where are the places I can turn to so that I might learn about my particular "stranger"? Who could help me find out more?

For Care Partners and Families
- What steps could we take to help our family member not be "perceived as being old"?

For Small Groups

- How might losses we have experienced provide us with "tastes of resurrection"?

- What have we learned about the life of a religious and of a religious community through the pages of this book? What has been important to apply to our lives in the broader community? In our congregation?

Postscript

A guided meditation given at a March 2002 meeting of the Diocesan Spiritual Direction Group here at St. John's House provided an image for all that had taken place in the preceding months. At first I resisted. I chafed against the shortening of our regular meditation time, the super-sweet music that was supposed to calm us, the prospect of fifteen minutes of talk when I wanted to sink into prayer with the psalm printed on our handouts.

The first words our leader spoke transfixed me: "No suffering touches us that has not first passed through the hands of God."

We were invited to walk along a mountain trail on a warm, sunny day. It took us through a meadow, with a creek bubbling along beside the trail. We were to enjoy the green meadow, the blue sky with its banks of ever-changing clouds, the songbirds, the warmth of the sun. Then, suddenly, we came to a bend in the trail. Before us was a mighty cataract, with thundering tons of water crashing every second down a steep rock face. This water would in time break off or wear away the hardest rock. Drenched to the bones by the spray, we managed to take refuge in a small cave.

I had already made the connection. Powerfully moved, I turned my attention to the psalm, to which the guided imagery meditation had been the prelude. "My tears have been my food day and night…. I went with the multitude and led them into the house of God, With the voice of praise and thanksgiving, among those who keep holy-day…. One deep calls to another in the noise of your cataracts; all your rapids and floods have gone over me …. Why are you so full of heaviness, O my soul? and why are you so disquieted within me? Put your trust in God; for I will yet give thanks to [the One who is], who is the help of my countenance, and my God" (*The Book of Alternative Services of the Anglican Church of Canada*, pp. 758–759).

As I took my place in the festive throng, I contrasted their shouts of joy and thanksgiving with the tears that had become my food day and night. Truly the waves and breakers had swept over me. Would the relentless force of the cataract erode the self-pity, self-dramatization, and self-concern of my rocky heart? Deep called to deep. This had gone deeper than I had ever imagined or intended.

I knew that when the time came for sharing, I must speak my truth. I did so, with a calm that surprised me. I spoke of my diagnosis. I told how, though physically and medically I was doing well, emotionally and spiritually I was being torn apart. I affirmed that, despite it all, I was able to hope and to praise. I said that the whole experience was a grace. I ended by saying once again that I cannot bear this burden alone. My words were received with the silent respect characteristic of our group. I knew I had been heard. I felt free. Free at last to move on.

Suggestions for Reflection/Discussion

For Individuals

- When did I encounter a serious turning-point in my life? Or have I found it yet?

For Care Partners and Families

- What happens if your family member's serious turning-point in life occurs at a time when you are at your lowest?

- How do you speak the truth, no matter what it is, to your family member? Or what is in the way of doing so?

For Small Groups

- While we cannot provide serious life-turning-points for others or for ourselves, how do we open ourselves to such possibilities?

Through the Gate

Except for a few bad days, brought on, typically, by my trying to drive myself the way I had when my health was sound, I continued to make good progress. I was doing all the right things. I walked daily. I followed a regular program of stretching and range of motion exercises. I strengthened muscle and bone by working with free weights. I watched my diet and made sure I got enough sleep. My sanguine mood continued. I would continue to go from strength to strength, and all would be well.

My journal entry for 15 December 2001 tells a different story:

> Today I walked through a gate and closed it behind me.
>
> Up until today, I was a detached, intellectual observer, trapped in a body/mind dualism. I read all I could, checking out what applied to me, somewhat bewildered at the expressions of shock, pain, and concern on the faces of friends to whom I blithely announced, "I have Parkinson's."
>
> Yesterday, as I climbed laboriously onto the table for a routine x-ray examination and even more laboriously turned over, the technician asked if I had back trouble. I replied, "I have Parkinson's—I'm a bit on the slow side."

I was saying this about *myself*, not just a body I happen to inhabit.

That evening, I had read an article, "Cognitive Changes Associated with Parkinson's Disease" (in *Caring for the Parkinson Patient*, J. Thomas Hutton and Raye Lynne Dippel, eds., 1999). The penny dropped. That was me they were talking about—and not just sometime down the road, but now. "Reduced ability to concentrate or 'think through' an activity.... Difficulty in finding a specific word one wants to use.... Loss of one's train of thought while speaking [well, sometimes] ... increased time required to process information ... increased distractibility and inattention, feeling overwhelmed when too much information is presented too fast"—I recognized them all. I learned that cognitive changes can take place in the early stages. There was no denying it: this was happening to me.

The further I read, the worse it became. There are reciprocal pathways—a sort of two-way street—between the basal ganglia in the mid-brain that control movement and the frontal lobe of the cortex, which enables language skills and reasoning powers. What happens in the cortex mirrors what happens in the mid-brain: slowness of thinking mirrors an underlying slowness of movement.

It all made sense. But what a blow to pride of intellect, to the illusion that I was so well endowed that a little loss would never be noticed! "In Parkinson's disease," I read on, "this results in individuals who are typically oriented, aware of surroundings, have understanding of time, and have general knowledge but are cognitively inefficient" (ibid., p. 154). Cognitively inefficient, I thought. *Who, me? Yes, you.*

Worse was to follow. I learned there is a 30 per cent chance that dementia may occur in the later stages—not the dementia of Alzheimer's, but a condition that "may be characterized more by a relative lack of aphasia [loss of verbal understanding or expression], more difficulty in retrieval of learned material (i.e., forgetfulness), slow problem solving, more personality and mood changes (i.e., depression and apathy), and prominent disturbances of gait and motor function" (ibid., p. 64).

With Parkinson's, everything is efficiently stored on the hard drive, but the software needed to retrieve it is in disarray.

⁂

I shed many a tear during the next few weeks—tears of grieving for what I had imagined would remain a guaranteed possession. Whatever happened to others, my mental powers would stay intact. My body would not outlive my mind.

Before long, however, I was drawn to a book that had been a turning-point for me in the 1960s, Pierre Teilhard de Chardin's *Le Milieu Divin*. I remembered how he had insisted that the fullest development of our human powers must precede any thought of sacrifice or self-abnegation.

> No sweet-smelling smoke without incense. No sacrifice without a victim. How would [we] give [ourselves] to God if [we] did not exist? What possession could [we] transfigure by [our] detachment if [our] hands were empty? (Pierre Teilhard de Chardin, *Le Milieu Divin*. London: Collins, 1960, p. 77)

Strenuous effort to maximize our human potential, far from setting us at odds with the Creator, would enable the divine plan for creation to be more fully realized through us. This was the "divinisation of our activities." Built into creation were also the "passivities of growth" that helped us on our way toward inward development and outward success, the "two hands of God" working in us to bring about the divine purpose for us, and through us.

I was aware, of course, that Teilhard also spoke about the passivities of diminishment—but all that, though eloquently presented, had seemed remote and abstract when I was an energetic woman in her thirties, aware of her abilities and delighting to use them in new and creative ways. Now I was impelled to immerse myself in Teilhard's reflections on diminishment.

The forces of diminishment, Teilhard states, lie both within us and outside us. Those outside us mean little to us because we can always imagine getting back what we have lost. "What is terrible for us is to be cut off from things through some inward diminishment that can never be retrieved" (ibid., p. 60).

> Humanly speaking, the internal passivities of diminishment form the darkest element and the most despairingly useless years of our life. Some were waiting to pounce on us as we first awoke.... Others were lying in wait for us later on and appeared as suddenly and brutally as an accident, or as stealthily as an illness.... And if by chance we escape ... there still remains that slow, essential deterioration which we cannot escape: old age little by little robbing us of ourselves and pushing us on toward the end.... In death, as in an ocean, all our slow or swift diminishments flow out and merge. (Ibid., pp. 60–61)

Now I was ready to hear about diminishment—too ready, perhaps. But Teilhard went on to bring growth and diminishment together in a robust and challenging synthesis. "No one has the right to say, 'God has touched me' without fighting the evil to the utmost of one's powers. The more we repel suffering at that moment, with our whole heart and our whole strength, the more closely we cleave to the heart and action of God" (Ibid., p. 62).

Eventually, however, we will be overcome. The time will come when we must let go. Yet the very "hostile force that lays [us] low and disintegrates [us] can become for [us] a loving principle of renewal, if [we accept] it with faith while never ceasing to struggle against it" (ibid., p. 72).

This leads, finally, to a "communion through diminishment":

When the signs of age begin to mark my body
(and still more when they touch my mind);
when the ill that is to diminish me or carry me off
strikes from without or is born within me;
when the painful moment comes in which I
    suddenly awake to the fact
that I am ill or growing old;
and above all at that last moment
when I feel I am losing hold of myself
and am absolutely passive
within the hands of the great unknown forces that
have formed me;
in all those dark moments, O God,
grant that I may understand that it is you
(provided only my faith is strong enough)
who are painfully parting the fibres of my being
in order to penetrate to the very marrow of my
    substance
and bear me away within yourself. (Ibid., p. 69)

So my agenda was set. Whatever the future might hold, my present task was to live as fully as was in my power.

It is not always easy to translate insight into action.

When I walked into my neurologist's office the morning of 14 December, she exclaimed, "Walking like a young girl!" She increased the Sinemet CR to three tablets a day, and asked me to come back toward the end of January. I left her office in a buoyant mood. That extra tablet would put me over the top, and I could enjoy my "dopamine honeymoon" for years to come.

I soon discovered that there were good days and bad days. I also learned that bad days became still worse when anxiety, stress, and fear took over. For the first time, insomnia and restless leg movements became a problem. On one occasion, I sat in my armchair for three-quarters of an hour or more, totally lacking the impetus to move.

On Christmas morning I played the organ at a Eucharist at St. Barnabas' Church. The twenty or so people who attended sat in the choir stalls, while Father Geoff Howson, immobilized by an ankle injury, sat in front of the sanctuary steps. I was deeply moved by Geoff's homily about the light shining in the darkness. "We are all light, and we are all darkness," he said. I thought how difficult it is for me to accept the darkness in those with whom I live and even more difficult to acknowledge my own. The insight came as I sat in tears, hidden from view (mercifully) by the console: "I can't carry this burden alone. I need the help of my Sisters."

Exhaustion caught up with me at intervals throughout the day. But I was also able to reflect on what was happening. I realized that the novelty and excitement of a new challenge, a new experience, had worn off. I recognized that I was grieving—for the person I had been, the hard worker with boundless energy for all kinds of projects, able to work for hours, pushing myself to the limits. I was also grieving over the cognitive changes already evident, and the likelihood of more to come. However, I did not rule out the possibility that depression, anxiety, or sheer fatigue might be making matters worse. I also acknowledged that inattentiveness and distractibility might be rooted in previously formed bad habits. I had been able to ignore this when my mind was agile and could operate on several tracks at a time. Not so now. Perhaps through this deficit, I thought, would come the hitherto elusive grace of one-pointed attention.

I acknowledged that pride was involved—the stoicism I had been brought up to admire and emulate; the belief that all signs of weakness were shameful; the independence I had fostered lifelong to protect my boundaries against violation; a determination, perhaps, to compensate for my small stature by great achievements; my effort to bind anxiety by strength of will and character. Underneath, the terrible conviction that self-disclosure would inevitably bring scorn and rejection.

There had also been a certain dramatization, and more than a little self-pity—a notion that nobody understood what I was going through. Wrong! It was true only if I didn't tell people of my experience. "I must risk exposure. I must use words and not rely on the observation of those around me. I can do it with God's help" I reflected, "but that help might come in very different ways than I expect or want. It might well come through this household."

In my journal I wrote, "I am still committed to the journey. I am still walking with God. But I now recognize the need for human companionship as well."

For several years I had experienced problems with singing—hoarseness and breaking of the voice in particular. Now I wondered why these problems persisted when everything else was going so well. My self-confidence was beginning to crumble. In my journal I wrote:

> I can walk now. I can't sing as I would wish. I had my heart set on being able to sing well again. Perhaps the time just hasn't come yet.... Don't push it.... If I can walk, why should I be unable to sing? It doesn't work that way!

> I am restless this morning. Can't settle down to rest or pray. Every word I read seems irrelevant, part of a world so remote that I can't even touch it. I am bound in a rigid body, immobilized spiritually and psychologically. "I am in prison and cannot get forth"—and I was doing so well.

> *Let go....* Yes, you are the God of my life.... I can't by anxiousness add a cubit to my stature—or a note to my voice. *Let go....* Entrust it all to God. Does it matter if I ever sing well again. It does to me. Does it to You? One more diminishment?

> Then, what about my vivid dream of the glorious black stallion—glossy coat, lithe limbs, ready to carry me, but drinking with me out of the same bathtub trough? I took it to mean that I was being given back energy and vitality. But I was also naked in the dream, while

people were holding clothes in front of me to protect me from others' gaze.

Must I then be stripped naked before that splendid energy can be released? Direct my ways, O God. To sing again—not now, but in your good time. Perhaps never again in this life.... I am weary beyond words. Drained. This whole business has been an emotional roller-coaster. And it is only the beginning.

This was a turning-point. Once I was able to accept the likelihood that my singing days were over, my morale became strong. I was able to laugh and enter into the life of the household. This was the first time I could recall when I was able to rise above symptoms and function well, without undue stress or anxiety. I learned to take time out when needed. I came to take the usual fluctuations in symptoms with an equilibrium that enabled me to deal with each day as it came.

My energy level increased steadily—so much so that from time to time I had to remind myself, and others, that I had limitations that must be respected. For a long time, I felt I had just enough energy to get through the day's activities. Now I had some left over for other things. I composed a trumpet descant for a service for which Sister Jean and I were providing the music. I took up sewing projects that had lain around for months. One Saturday I and Alice Kudo, my friend for over fifty years, spent two hours on foot exploring parts of Pointe St-Charles near where she lives. I got in touch with Annie Lavigne of the Parkinson Society Québec, and plans for an Anglophone support group on the South Shore got underway.

I felt I had moved ahead. Realizing that in my preoccupation with health issues I had become apathetic toward the sufferings of the world, I was ready to look beyond myself. I looked forward to resuming former interests and activities, and exercising my creative powers.

Suggestions for Reflection/Discussion

For Individuals
- How do I manage the balance between accepting my diminishing capacities and pushing myself to do what I can?

- Am I missing certain ways that would allow me to walk my pathway through life as a channel of grace?

For Care Partners and Families
- Learn as much as you can about the grieving process. Name your feelings or "where you are" at any given moment. Naming where you are helps give you some power over what is happening.
Understand that your family member may be at a turning-point, and others who love you at another point.

- How can you help your family member feel more "at home" with whoever she/he is and wherever she/he is?

For Small Groups
- Most of us understand grieving related to death and dying. Elizabeth Kubler-Ross wrote very helpful material to launch this topic in conversation. But what seems different about grieving related to aging, or to a chronic illness that seems to get better and then worse again?

- What do we need to learn about "being at home"? How can we help each other learn to be comfortable with ourselves?

The Long Haul Begins

O God,
when you give to us your servants
any great matter to do,
grant us also to know
that it is not the beginning,
but the continuing of it
until it is thoroughly finished,
which yields the true glory
through him
who for the finishing of your work
laid down his life,
our redeemer, Jesus Christ.
Amen.

"You will have it for a long time," my neurologist remarked, commenting on her decision to leave my medication unchanged in order to forestall possible side-effects and to maintain me at a "functional" level. I wrote in my journal in January 2002:

> I came to my appointment with an array of symptoms. Some are minor annoyances—that, and no more. Much more serious is the debilitating fatigue that overwhelms me when I stretch my powers of concentration beyond a safe limit, or ride on a wave

of emotion, whether exhilarating or distressing. I still struggle against my addiction to work and the "lust to finish," and I still ignore the warning signs of fatigue, which can come when I sit too long at the computer, when I try to cram too much work into a day, or even when I begin to feel tired on a long walk and insist on going farther.

And then there is still the spectre of cognitive decline. Although my neurologist told me "not to worry about all that," I am haunted, at times, by an image of my frontal lobes being sucked, bit by bit, down into the black void of my mid-brain.

I often felt that people had not grasped the reality of my situation. When our Reverend Mother sent round a report on various Sisters' health that described me as my "old energetic and creative self," I was dismayed. I wrote her a long letter expressing my fear that people would expect the same level of energy and competency I once had.

For a while I had felt a renewal of energy. I was learning to take the "bad days" in my stride. Before long, however, a prolonged and painful situation in our household escalated, and this undermined my sense of well-being. It took several months for me to recover, physically, emotionally, and spiritually. The experience taught me the extent to which emotional stress can worsen symptoms. Likewise, my improvement, after the painful situation was resolved, convinced me that what I took to be the irreversible progression of the disease was a temporary response to a severe emotional trauma.

One thing I needed to work out was a balance between openness and reserve about my condition. I had to get over the attitude of not wanting to call attention to myself. At the other extreme, I had to resist the lure of what I call the "Ancient Mariner syndrome," the temptation to hold unwary inquirers after my health with a glittering eye and tell them everything I know about my condition. Gradually, having regained perspective regarding my life as a whole, I no longer felt the compulsion to talk about Parkinson's, but was happy to do so when the opportunity came to educate or to comfort.

Meanwhile, I was working toward bringing to birth the South Shore Anglophone Support Group. Taking flyers around to churches, seniors' residences, and public buildings, and above all, advertising in the local St-Lambert Journal, brought responses. So it was that on 12 March 2002 about twenty people appeared ("out of nowhere," as one of our resident guests put it) for the first meeting. About a dozen people had pre-registered in response to the advertising, and the rest just showed up. Annie Lavigne from the Parkinson Society Québec was there to speak about the work of the society. I had a carefully planned agenda, with a flip chart and other adjuncts of a well-run meeting, but it soon became clear that people's greatest need was to make connections and just talk.

Who were these people? There were married couples, one being the care partner. There were people with Parkinson's who came on their own. And there were spouses of those who were not well enough to come. Good connections were established. A woman whose husband had just been diagnosed found support from one whose husband had lived with Parkinson's for thirty years. Understandably, the group did not meet the needs of everyone. Two or three people came and did not return; one, just diagnosed, said she was not ready to deal with some distressing things she had heard about the progression of the disease.

It was good to be able to speak a common language, without the need of elaborate explanations. When one woman lost her balance and almost fell off her chair, nobody made a fuss—it could have happened to any of us. It was good, too, to be able to laugh together, as we did when a woman, describing the effects of a well-known dopamine agonist on her husband, grimaced and exclaimed, "Forget Viagra!"

The meetings continued throughout the spring in a relatively unstructured way, and people seemed content. When we reconvened in the fall, we felt a need for outside speakers. This sparked new energy and enthusiasm. For a while, we had a member who gave us an exercise period at the beginning of meetings. From time to time we had meetings at which people with Parkinson's and care partners met separately. Meetings ran from 2:00 to 4:00 P.M., with a tea break in the middle, to which some or all of the Sisters came.

The last meeting of the spring session was a pot-luck and barbecue—a happy event held indoors because of rainy weather. Counting the Sisters and house guests, there were about two dozen people. All went well, even though we had a tense moment when the gentlemen doing the barbecuing on the verandah managed to incinerate three hamburgers. Smoke filled the adjoining refectory, but promptly closed doors prevented the alarm system from going off and bringing fire trucks to the door!

I continued to have happy contacts with the downtown office of Parkinson Society Québec, and to be involved in such activities as the annual Parkinson's conference and the Super-Walk, their signature fund-raising event. A by-product has been greater confidence in speaking French. Emerging from a Christmas party for staff and volunteers, I felt as if I had spent the previous two hours in a French immersion class!

~~~~~

The first time I recognized that the moment had come to relinquish an activity that had become important to me over the years was when I decided to give up leadership of the retreat I had led for the Toronto Chapter of Integrity (Gay and Lesbian Anglicans and their Friends) for more than twenty years. During the 1970s I had become aware of the discrimination, on the part of both the church and society, against people with a same-sex orientation. As a sign of solidarity, I had offered the Toronto Chapter of Integrity my experience as a retreat conductor. From time to time I also wrote articles for their newsletter, *The Integrator*.

In 2001 I had been deeply dissatisfied with the retreat I offered. The preparation was laborious, and the result seemed to be cobbled together from various sources without a central theme. Preparation a year later was still more taxing. Several times I was on the point of giving up. Only the offer of Chris Ambidge, a friend, a long-time member of Integrity, and a persistent advocate for fair treatment of gays and lesbians, to share the leadership emboldened me to keep on. I grasped at the offer, and sent him what I had prepared thus far—poor, incoherent fragments they seemed to me. However, Chris liked the ideas, and we agreed to collaborate. So we did our preparation together by e-mail, and on the Friday afternoon before the retreat began, we put the final touches on the retreat addresses.

The retreat went well, thanks to Chris's help. The theme,

"Strangers in our Midst," held the interest of the group, and I found the confidence to rework the four addresses into a series of articles for *The Integrator*.

On the second afternoon, it was clear that a speech was about to be made, a heart-warming expression of appreciation for all the years I had led the retreat. The presentation of an attractive waterproof sports jacket followed—"So you can think of us when you're out walking." With it was a card with warm expressions of affection and appreciation. Later there came an envelope of money for a shrub for the garden in Montreal. I was particularly moved by the applause that greeted my announcement that I intended to keep coming to the retreats. "We'll move the retreat to the Infirmary when the time comes!" participants said.

I found I was able to let go peacefully, with a sense of rightness. I had done my grieving. Best of all, I knew that these people were my friends and that the friendship would continue. I didn't have to be an expert or a fountain of wisdom; I was loved and accepted for myself, whatever my limitations.

Another major issue has been learning to accept help graciously and without taking advantage of people's kindness. Because of a busy season and an unexpected journey to western Canada, I found myself facing a deadline I could not possibly meet. My task was to collate a large volume of questionnaires from Oblates and Sisters, which were to form the basis of my report to General Chapter as Oblate Director—precisely the type of detailed work that overwhelms me and brings on fatigue. I asked for the help I needed and got it. Sister Sue and I worked our way through the material, usually for an hour at a time, which was all that I could manage. We got most of it done before I had to leave for the west and Sue went on holiday.

On my return, I was able to complete the rest without undue pressure and to distill the salient points into a coherent summary. By August, realizing that I could not do justice to my responsibilities as Oblate Director, and to the demands of a busy branch house, I asked to be relieved of the Oblate work.

⁂

"You've heard of motion sickness?" I liked to say. "Well, this is slow motion sickness." I have been blessed with a sense of humour, and the grave issues I have wrestled with have done nothing to quench it. Sometimes, comic relief comes from situations like this:

My departure from the Gare Centrale en route to Toronto was hilarious. When we arrived in front of the main entrance, the official on duty told us that we could not park there. Sister Anitra, the driver, explained, "I have to take her baggage in—she has Parkinson's. Seeing that this had no effect, she tried again: "She has *Parkinson's!*" The official then assured us that I could have a wheelchair. (At this stage, I was still walking pretty well, so I murmured to Anitra, "Let's make this good—come and help me get out of the car," and with her "help" I hobbled out and over to a bench near the main entrance. Along came a redcap with a wheelchair, and from there he wheeled me over to the pre-boarding area, where he left me sitting for the next half-hour. Conveniently, the tremor in my right leg kicked in, which made my condition look more convincing! I did feel a bit of a fraud as other passengers no more mobile than myself arrived on foot; but part of me was enjoying the situation. When boarding time arrived, my redcap reappeared, took me down the escalator in the wheelchair, and put me on the train. I barely resisted the temptation to wave at the other passengers, who were still waiting their turn. Once we were on board, the redcap showed me my luggage and asked, "Can you walk?" I assured him that I could.

When I detrained in Toronto, I carried my bags unaided to the clock outside Union Station (the rendezvous for Sisters meeting trains), and stood waiting in the rain. I couldn't help thinking, "It's a good thing that redcap in Montreal can't see me now!"

Nevertheless, I have been glad to take advantage of Air Canada's wheelchair service on the flights to western Canada I have made since then. Even though I could have walked, using a wheelchair enabled me to travel with a minimum of fatigue.

One last original one-liner: My computer is getting so slow that I think it must have Parkinson's!

There have been sombre moments as well.

Early in June 2002 swallowing began to be a problem, and I had to learn a new way of eating. (An interesting side-benefit has been the shedding of ten surplus pounds.) The wake-up call came during a steak dinner in the hall of the local parish, when I tried to swallow a large piece of gristle. I should have known better. The piece blocked my windpipe, and all I could do was gasp, "I'm choking!" In what I can only describe as divine providence, it turned out that I was sitting next to a man who had just completed first-aid training. In an instant he was behind me, performing the Heimlich manoeuvre. The gristle popped up into my mouth and I could breathe. Never shall I forget the feel of the cool air flowing back into my lungs—the very breath of life!

My singing voice was becoming increasingly undependable. There was a time when I worried if I couldn't produce a beautiful tone; now I was thankful to be able to sing at all. One day, when our strongest singers were absent from choir, my voice gave out. Sister Helena, aged 84, stepped in as cantor and sang the litany very well. So there we were, three elders, gallantly glorifying God with whatever voice we had—and I felt peaceful about being one of them.

There have been many moments of comfort and inspiration: as a Sister leaves for her holiday, one of the two friends who have come for her gives me a hug and says, "Glad to see you looking *so well*." "You know about me?" She nods in reply. Nothing more needs to be said; I know that I am known—and understood.

Another such moment: that summer, for several weeks Sister Beryl and I pay regular hospital visits to the husband of a woman in our support group, who is recovering from broken bones resulting from a fall. Gradually, superficial conversation deepens. I am asked one evening if I have found God in my experience with Parkinson's. This leads to deep and nourishing conversation.

And another moment: a retired bishop, Stuart Payne, staying at our house, tells a story that sums up for me what has happened during the last several months, and what lies ahead. It is about a school race. At one end of the starting line is a strong, athletic boy, a born winner. At the other is a small, scrawny lad who doesn't stand a chance. The race begins, and of course the first boy wins. Indeed, he sets a new record and is roundly cheered. Most of the other boys have dropped out, and the officials are already clearing things away when the scrawny lad staggers in and collapses in the ashes, bruising and bloodying his face. "Why didn't you give up?" the official asks. The lad replies, "When the boy who was supposed to come was unable, the teacher asked me." "But you knew you couldn't win." "I wasn't told to win. I wasn't told to quit. I was told to run the race."

Suggestions for Reflection/Discussion

For Individuals
- How do I decide when the time has come to withdraw from a responsibility or activity that has been important to me?

For Care Partners and Families
- How do you give support to your family member while respecting his/her autonomy?

For Small Groups
- What kind of support would you offer a close friend with a chronic, progressive illness? What kind of support would you offer that person's family?

A Journey Just Begun

For behold, you look for truth deep within me,
and will make me understand wisdom secretly....
Make me hear of joy and gladness,
that the body you have broken may rejoice....
Create in me a clean heart, O God,
and renew a right spirit within me.
Cast me not away from your presence
and take not your holy Spirit from me.
Give me the joy of your saving help again
and sustain me with your bountiful Spirit.

(Psalm 51, *The Book of Alternative Services*)

In his *Prayer Companions' Handbook,* John Wickham, SJ, speaks of our life stages and the transitions we make from one stage to the next. Reading what Wickham has to say about the transition from mid-life to seniority helped pinpoint where I was in my own life. Wickham cites the "signs of one's own weakened health, energies and desires" as factors that may set the transition process in motion:

> Perhaps one does not have the same resources to call upon that one used to take for granted. Some ... will disregard these indications and at this stage make greater efforts than before to achieve in the world what they have long ambitioned. That is, they try to prolong

their Mid-life tendency to believe in themselves and their special goals in life.... Others will see it, even if they themselves refuse to do so. (John Wickham, SJ. Montreal: Ignatian Centre Publications, 3rd ed., 1991, p. 134)

Stressful though the transition may be, the fruits of the struggle are precious:

Other forms of realization may swim into one's ken, much to one's surprise. And once these are accepted, they may seem to be the best of all. (Ibid., p. 134)

Wickham mentions three gifts:

Detachment—"a certain distance from the main roles in society ... which the individual may have attained formerly in one degree or another";

Holy wisdom—"Many years of reflection upon one's lifelong experiences in the light of faith may be an essential component of the special gift which each individual may attain"; and

"*Failing faculties*, such as crippled limbs, poor eyesight, loss of hearing or lessened energy, may become the occasion of the very best contributions of a spiritual kind" that the senior can make. (Ibid., p. 139)

On reflection, I recognized a connection between the transition from mid-life to seniority and the anxiety and angry impatience with myself that had bedevilled me in those several years before my diagnosis, an unconscious resistance to the inevitable aging process. Because I had enjoyed good health and abundant energy, I had been able to prolong my "middle age" mode of living into my early seventies. Even after a year of living with Parkinson's, I found it hard to give up old ways. For long afterwards I would push myself beyond my limits, despite knowing I would pay the price in anxiety and fatigue.

Seen in retrospect, events I would not have chosen to live through have proved to be the means of grace. A Sister in our household was suffering from major depression and anxiety, and unexplored vulnerabilities in my own personality drew me into an emotional maelstrom. Reflecting in my journal sometime later, I wrote:

> I felt that I had been traumatized by the depth of the pain I had experienced to the extent that I was still feeling the effects. This experience and that of coming to terms with Parkinson's reinforced each other. I might have been able to deal with one or the other, but having the two converge was too much. The impact of the situation made my symptoms worse and that, in turn, made me less able to cope with pain, stress, and anxiety.

While at our cottage in the summer of 2002, I started to read Thomas Keating's writings on centering prayer. He speaks of such prayer as an act of consent to the presence and activity of God—a presence that affirms and heals, and an activity that draws up from the depths of the unconscious the poison of wounds that have lain hidden and festering from birth onward, and in so doing, enables the death of the "false self," which we develop to protect ourselves from the raw, unbearable pain.

The false self operates through "emotional programs for happiness" designed to satisfy the needs for power, control, acceptance, esteem, and security that, by their very nature, are left unfulfilled for the baby and young child lacking the life experience and cognitive development to understand its situation. The child experiences this lack of fulfilment as a rejection of its own personhood, a deep wound that, hidden perhaps for a lifetime, secretly and destructively drives behaviour. So it may happen that an adult of seventy harbours a two-year-old whose rage can ruin relationships and cause tremendous pain both to oneself and to others. It became clear to me that my pain and my response to the situation I have described stemmed from an unrecognized program of happiness based on my unfulfilled need for acceptance and esteem.

It was with gratitude that I received the insight that even the agony that the situation had caused me was part of my healing:

> My diagnosis and the process of dealing with it, the situation in the household and the turmoil it evoked, and my discovery of the writings of Thomas Keating, form a single, threefold cord. All three strands have passed through the hands of God, who has woven them into one in order to draw me out of lifelong destructive patterns and pull me Godward.

A sure sign of grace received has been a measure of healing in the relationship between me and the other Sister. Each of us had followed our own lonely journey, unable to recognize the depth of the other's desperate struggle because of our own. Now our friendship could reach a deeper level in the acknowledgement of the common path we had trod.

⁓

The final grace in this year of grace came through the Long Retreat at our Mother House, led by Margaret Silf, whose many books, based on Ignatian spirituality, have been widely read in our community.

I didn't know what to expect from Margaret, but felt it would be stupid to throw away the opportunity to hear her. I found her both warm and profound. Her images and the stories she told evoked deep responses in me. I struggled with the usual issues, trying by a desperate act of will to make the total surrender against which my whole being mobilized itself.

Then the insight was given to me in prayer that this surrender was impossible for me to make by my own efforts and in my own strength:

> Come to me, all you that are *weary* and are *carrying heavy burdens*, I will *give* you *rest* [not effort, not performance, not achievement, but *rest*]. Take my yoke upon you, and *learn* from me ... and you will find rest ... for my yoke is *easy*, and my burden is *light*." (Matthew 11:28–30)

And then, Margaret suggested that, though Jesus was restricted to one particular set of circumstances in his human life—for example, he did not know what it is to be a woman, to be married, to be old and infirm—he wants to experience and redeem all these circumstances through the life of each one of us, and will do so if we are willing. (My first reaction was, "Hey! Jesus has Parkinson's!") Margaret used the image of a pathway given to each of us, a challenge to respond to Christ's call and gift to enable us to live the unique vocation he has given us, and in so doing, take into his consciousness yet another aspect of human life. In the notes of her addresses are the following words:

> Each of us walks one pathway through life, and that pathway is unique. If I do not walk it in a way that makes me a channel of grace, no one ever will.... My particular track, traced through my life's events, my relationships, my unique mix of gifts and weaknesses ... is becoming a channel of God's redeeming love, if I am willing to live through, with, and in God.

Next, Margaret proposed the following exercise: "In my life, right now, Christ is redeeming in me what it means to be ..."

> ... a seventy-four year old woman
> with Parkinson's
> an Anglican Sister
> a musician and a writer, a walker and a sew-er
> a supporter of lesbians and gays in the church and in society
> a friend, for whom friendships are important and life-giving
> a nine on the Enneagram and an INFP on the Myers-Briggs type indicator
> a thoroughly self-centred and self-protective human being.

Christ is redeeming all that!

Then I did an exercise that invited me to chart the "shape, direction, and terrain of my own pathway." In doing this, I discerned that my pathway had been going around in circles, with myself as the centre around which the circles kept revolving. In desperation, I breathed a prayer, "Jesus, *you* take over!"

I recall vividly a day when, after a morning of interruptions and unforeseen demands and ten minutes before a French Eucharist in our chapel, I discovered that I had not made enough leaflets for those present. Furthermore, in the midst of it all, I had to use the washroom and take my Sinemet. By the time I reached the chapel, I had visibly "lost it." I was shedding tears of self-reproach, with tremors both inside and out, but the household understood, and graciously upheld me through it all.

Such painful experiences are necessary reminders of my limitations. They leave me feeling stripped and naked, just as I was in the dream I recounted earlier. As in the dream, my Sisters "covered my nakedness" by their empathy and silent support. It would take me a long time for the energy I expended in blaming and castigating myself to be transformed into the vitality and wholesome energy represented in my dream by the black stallion.

It is still hard for me to accept how fragile and vulnerable I am, despite my efforts to order and control my life. Perhaps the people I live with see my needs and my limitations more clearly than I, and show me the compassion and acceptance that I have not yet been able to show myself. If so, it is a gift I have not yet acknowledged, preoccupied as I have been with my own harsh demands and glittering expectations. It is a

humbling lesson to learn, after a lifetime of fierce independence and self-sufficiency, but learn it I must.

When I was at the convent in Toronto early in 2003 to take
part in a workshop on Celtic spirituality, Sister Constance
Joanna asked me if I would consider returning to the convent
later in the year. I gave the matter some thought, then agreed
to return. It was not an easy decision. Yes, I had been happy in
our Montreal house; it was also the scene of one of the most
significant events of my life—my diagnosis and all that had
flowed from it in self-knowledge and spiritual growth. I knew,
however, that the life and ministry of a busy branch house
required four Sisters in robust health, able to take their full
share in an increasingly demanding ministry.

My return to the Mother House was delayed for a year.
During this time, I was aware of changes in my condition,
but they were very gradual. Generally speaking, I had more
stamina than before and was able to work at the computer for
longer stretches without mental and physical fatigue. When I
did need to take a rest, I recovered more quickly. I was able to
take on the project of writing a substantial essay for publication in a collection, Living Together in the Church (edited by Chris
Ambidge and Greig Dunn, ABC Publishing, 2004).

I was fortunate enough to be accepted as a patient of Dr.
Anne-Louise Lafontaine, director of the Movement Disorder
Clinic at the Montreal Neurological Institute. I had heard Dr.
Lafontaine speak on two occasions, and had been impressed
by her expert knowledge and warm personality. Her skilful
fine-tuning of my medications from time to time enabled
me to live with a minimum of symptoms. I cannot speak
too highly of Dr. Lafontaine and her team. Not only are they

experts in their fields: they welcome you, listen to you, and take you seriously.

I ceased to worry about cognitive changes. Indeed, my biggest problem was the need to remind my household of my limitations—a sure sign that I was doing well. One day Sister Jean and I reached an impasse in a conversation that had been moving at cross-purposes, and I lost patience. I expostulated, "I'm on overload. You know I can't cope when you give me information so fast. I can't process it!" She replied, "You're so sharp that I forget you have these limitations." My next move was to photocopy an article on cognitive changes from the *Parkinson Post* and give it to the Sisters to read. Never miss an opportunity to educate your household!

Sometime during the summer of 2003, I began to festinate—not constantly, but fairly regularly at certain times of the day, or when my medication was wearing off. This running with rapid little steps and forward-tilted posture provided another learning experience for both me and my household. The first time it happened publicly was when, to the surprise of all present, I moved toward the buffet for my supper as though released from a slingshot. Once the household got used to it, they took my festination for granted. Later on, a further adjustment in the timing of my medication made festination a rare occurrence and also dealt with the nuisance of nightly restless leg movements.

My household has been unfailingly supportive. They respect my needs, including my need for humour. I recognize the danger of humour becoming a form of denial or a way to distance oneself from pain or emotional anguish. At the same time, I am convinced that humour helps one to cope. Early in December we Sisters attended the Christmas party at the Montreal Diocesan Theological College. After an evening of good food and a well-topped-up sherry, I was feeling exuberant. I was trying to quote from a card in my wallet: "I'm not intoxicated; I have a neurological condition...." This in itself provoked a good deal of merriment—still more when I wove my way down the front steps of the "Dio," supported by Sister Beryl on one side and Sister Sarah Jean on the other.

A day or so later, I was having a bad time, and in my impatience, spoke sharply to Sister Jean. I apologized at once—one thing I have learned from living in a branch house is not to harbour anger until it sours into resentment. Sister Jean responded with a hug and said, "It's your neurological condition." Her sensitive response melted any anger that may have lingered. This episode was just one of many that made me aware of my Sisters' forbearance and compassion. It would be a long time before I showed similar compassion toward myself—longer still before I discovered that the anger I showed toward myself as well as others was the product of frustrated perfectionism.

⸙

During the last month or so of my time at Maison St-Jean, as I made preparations to move to the Mother House in Toronto, my focus began to shift. At the outset, my guiding metaphor was that of a journey. Little by little, and especially after I knew that I would be moving back to the Mother House, images of home and homecoming began to emerge. Although Maison St-Jean and the Sisters with whom I lived had been my home and family for over three years, I began to look forward to moving back to the convent in Toronto as homecoming in a deeper sense, a return to the place where I had spent by far the greater part of my adult life, and the place to which I was being called to new circumstances and new growth. I knew that my time in the Botham Road convent would be short;

we would be moving to a newly built convent, which in time we would take to our hearts as home.

Homecoming and journeying remain in tension. To find a home is to begin a new kind of journey. Home is a place where you can be yourself, and that commits you to find out and to share with your household, at ever deepening levels, who you really are. Even at home, especially at home, the journey of the spirit goes on. I begin to recognize that wherever my journey leads, I am at home in a very real sense, and have been so right along. It is a matter of "knowing the place for the first time," as T. S. Eliot expresses it. God knows us at a depth that we can never fathom, and welcomes us with an intensity and steadfastness of love we can never have for ourselves. And so we find the trust and the courage to continue the quest, even as we remain at home —precisely because we are at home and have been all along. In the embrace of the Triune God, journey and homecoming coalesce.

In *Christ on Trial: How the Gospel Unsettles our Judgment* (ABC Publishing, 2000), a remarkable book that both nourishes and challenges the reader, Rowan Williams explores the idea of "being at home" as it is developed in St. John's gospel:

We are not—it seems—permitted to be at home in the sense that we can feel ultimately satisfied with where and what we are, longing to hold on to it and unwilling to respond to challenge; we are not to settle down in our place and our time because we feel comfortable. There are always questions to be asked by us and of us. That said, however, what is asked of us is a commitment to the here and now—our questioning can never be an attempt to deny or to escape the present moment. To know this moment, this place, this body, this set of memories, this situation, for what it truly is and to accept this as reality, the reality with which God at each new instant begins to work: this is the "being at home" we have to learn. (pp. 84–85)

In John's gospel, Jesus promises to those who love him and keep his word that the Father will love them and "we will make our home with them." To be at home is to be in community. In community we both receive and give hospitality. Ultimately, it is in the community and hospitality of the Blessed Trinity that we find ourselves to be at home, and know beyond all knowing that we have always been at home in God even when we believed ourselves to be far away.

Suggestions for Reflection
(and sharing, as you are comfortable)

For Individuals, Families, and Care Partners
- As an individual, a family member, or as part of a study group, read and ponder the quotation from Margaret Silf's retreat, beginning, "Each of us walks one pathway through life..." (pp. 57–58 in this book).

Do one or both of these exercises:
- "In my life, right now, Christ is redeeming in me what it means to be [in my current state]." Explore the measure of truth in this statement.

- Consider and chart the shape, direction, and terrain of your own pathway.

Complete these exercises in silence, or share what feels comfortable for you.

Healing Where There Is No Cure

God of compassion and love.
We offer you all our suffering and pain.
Give us strength to bear our weakness,
healing even when there is no cure,
peace in the midst of turmoil,
and love to fill the spaces in our lives.

Although there is yet no cure for Parkinson's Disease, I can testify to many healings that have taken place, or are in progress, in my life. Some of these have resulted in friendships restored; others (which take longer and meet with more resistance) have to do with the entrenched habits and attitudes of a lifetime. In every such healing I can only rejoice and marvel at the goodness and patience of God.

For at least twenty-five years, it has been my custom to send a Christmas newsletter to my friends. It is an opportunity not only to bring them up to date on my doings, but to respond to the letters they have sent me. In replying to the 2001 newsletter from my friends Sue and Art Lawson, I wrote at some length about my recent diagnosis and its impact on my life. I hoped for some acknowledgement—after all, Art had been living with Parkinson's for years—but no reply came. I kept wondering, "What did I say that might have offended them?" Was I too brash? A bit too cheery about the whole thing? When I reread what I had written, I could find nothing that I would consider offensive.

Then I thought back to the last time I had seen Art, and how uncomfortable I had been seeing him so incapacitated. He must have sensed my discomfort. Perhaps he and Sue were thinking, "She could barely endure being in [Art's] presence for five minutes, and now she comes looking for sympathy?" I lived with this misery for several months, until during the Long Retreat of 2002 I was moved to write a letter, from which I quote the relevant parts:

> To come right to the point, [a recent] visit to the [Church of the] Redeemer brought into focus the last time we met. It was at the launching of *Common Praise*. You were there in a wheelchair, and I had a brief conversation with you. You were having difficulty with your speech that day, and I realize now that my hearing had already begun to deteriorate. (I wear hearing aids now.) I did not handle it well .... I panicked and excused myself with some trivial remark.... Because of your physical limitations ... I could not see that you were the same person I had known for so long, whose friendship had meant so much to me. I have to say, to my shame and sorrow, that I could not come to realize how callous and hurtful my behaviour was, and how much I too was the loser by it, until I had begun to walk the same path that you have travelled these many years. I ask your forgiveness.

I waited in vain for a reply. Would it have been better for me to have kept my repentance to myself? I wanted to see Art, and every time we Sisters, en route to the convent, passed Cobourg, where Art lived in a retirement residence, I felt a pang and offered a prayer. Finally, in May 2003, the opportunity came.

Sister Jean suggested that we stop for supper at Cobourg. My heart sank. I said, "How about Port Hope?" In the silence of my mind and heart, I knew how much I wanted to see Art, and how I dreaded the encounter. I prayed for courage, repeating the Holy Name again and again. Then, before I could change my mind, I blurted out, "Let's eat in Cobourg." Uncertain of the outcome, I kept on praying silently, my heart racing: *Perhaps I'll not say anything about a visit; but if I don't ask, I'll be throwing away what I have longed and prayed for so long.* So, having prepared the words carefully beforehand, I made bold to say, "Jean, I'd like to ask a favour"—and made my request. I had burned my bridges.

We ate in a pleasant restaurant and then drove to the retirement home. We found Art sitting alone in the dining room, doing the crossword puzzle from the local newspaper. He was overjoyed to see us. I was grateful that Providence had arranged things so that there were three of us Sisters—Jean, Helena, and myself. Amid the light-hearted conversation, Art said to me, quietly, "I haven't answered your letter yet; I want to give it the consideration it deserves." Our eyes met. My eyes were searching his. All was well; no more needed to be said. The others had no idea of the momentous thing that had passed between us.

We had a glorious visit. Art positively scintillated. I went away deeply happy and at peace. Later I reflected on what a role model Art is for me: he has not let his illness become an obsession, nor does he hide or minimize it. He has a zest for life; he delights in the accomplishments of his grown children; he can laugh. He keeps his mind alert—he knows what is happening in the larger world, as well as in his immediate circle. He can take delight in what each moment brings. And all this, after living with Parkinson's for eighteen years.

After this visit, whenever we drove past Cobourg, I felt a

sense of joy and gratitude, and said a prayer of thanksgiving for the brave man living there who was still my friend.

The friendship did not have an opportunity to ripen. Some years ago, Art had undergone a pallidotomy, surgery that restores mobility and reduces symptoms in those with advanced Parkinson's. The surgery had brought immediate relief—"resurrection," he had said at the time—but the benefits were not lasting. In his Christmas 2003 newsletter, Art expressed great hope at the prospect of deep brain stimulation, to take place in mid-January. This procedure would enable him to be more mobile, have less pain and discomfort, and be free from the constant shaking and freezing. He wrote:

> Now the big change is going to be for me.... I continue to be hopeful and positive about the chance for a renewed life. The best result we can hope for includes the possibility that I might once again be able to live at home with Sue ... and the other big change that is ahead of us is Sue's (and my?) move to the condo in Cobourg that is rising from the sodden ground as we write.

I was blessed with the opportunity to talk with Art and Sue by telephone the Saturday before his surgery. It was a good conversation, with laughter, symptom-swapping, and the hope of a "Shaker get-together" when Art was well enough. Art was admitted on the evening of 18 January and went to the operating room the next morning with humour and a real sense of calm. All went well at first, and Art was fully conscious, as is necessary in this procedure; but about two hours before the end, he fell into a profound sleep, from which he did not awake. He developed pneumonia and other complications. The next two weeks were a series of hopes repeatedly raised and dashed.

The family faced the situation with a strong and realistic faith. In one of her daily e-mail reports to a wide circle of friends, Sue wrote, "I'm convinced that Art's body and his spirit will make the decision about how hard to struggle. And I trust him so deeply to make the right decision. So, I worry about nothing and know it will be somehow fine."

Art died peacefully around noon on 31 of January. Sue wrote, "It's a huge loss for all of us, but you well know that he left a magnificent legacy of stories, of laughter, of wisdom, of courage behind him for us all to stand in awe of, and try to emulate in our futures."

Sister Elizabeth Ann and I attended the funeral, which was at St. Peter's Anglican Church, Cobourg, on Wednesday, 4 February. It was a magnificent occasion, and I felt privileged to be there. Readings, hymns, and a splendid homily all combined to convey a sense of Art's presence among us. At the same time, there was a sense of his being solidly established in the joy of the Life beyond.

The following Friday it was my privilege to play the organ in our convent chapel at the funeral of another priest associate of ours, Bill Wigmore. I played with a grace and freedom, a sense of the music being played *through* me, such as I had never experienced before. Several people later remarked on it. I can't help feeling that Art's "dancing" in the heavenly places, and *without* the devil on his back, had something very substantial to do with the grace I was given. So, though I never received his promised letter, and no opportunity came for us to resume our friendship fully, Art was able, in the communion of saints, to transmit a gift of affirmation and encouragement, an invigorating challenge to run with renewed resolution, courage, and joy, the race set before me.

My mother was convinced that she had Parkinson's. I did not question this until, during her final illness, her family doctor denied it. He said she had "a senile tremor."

My relationship with my mother had been difficult. We were opposites in temperament. When I was a child, I felt I could never meet her high standards, and during adolescence our relationship was turbulent. The only period in our lives in which we related as friends and mature women was from 1975 to 1980, when I was in my forties and in charge of our branch house in Edmonton. In her old age my mother suffered a distressing personality change. As her control slipped, her shadow side emerged and all the mean, critical, and sarcastic comments she had once suppressed were now freely expressed. She openly ridiculed my sister, her care partner, in the presence of guests. As for me, she brought up things from my past to embarrass me, and drew a picture of my life in the convent that was totally unreal. "You Sisters," she sneered, "are very *important*. You sit around all day while people wait on you"—a judgement she would never have made when she was in her right mind.

Although I was with my mother for only a week or two each year, as part of my holiday, the time spent together was enough to reopen old wounds. Returning to the convent after a particularly hard visit, I agreed readily to our Reverend Mother's suggestion that I go into therapy.

After my own diagnosis, such was my resentment, that I took comfort in the doctor's verdict that she did not have Parkinson's. I felt that if she had lived long enough to know that I had received the same diagnosis, she would have missed no opportunity to show me how much better she was at handling it than I. Or perhaps she would have said—with a measure of justice—"Now you know what it feels like!"

However, the longer I live with Parkinson's, the more similarities with my mother I find and the more symptoms I recognize. Tremor was the most obvious, but there were others. Rigidity, certainly: the time came when, too stiff to get into her daytime clothes, my mother bought a wardrobe of hostess gowns. Balance? She fell frequently, and I marvelled that she never broke a bone. Sleep disturbances? She gradually developed a pattern of turning night into day. Voice difficulties? Little by little she lost her voice and finally could barely speak above a whisper. Festination? She would run back and forth, back and forth, during the night, with rapid little steps and forward-tilted posture. She developed a grim Parkinsonian mask. Her loss of weight was startling.

My mother endured all these symptoms without the help of medication. Early on, she told me, she had "not responded" to the medication that was specific to Parkinson's. What this was, I do not know; by the early 1970s, levodopa was already in use. In any case, my respect for my mother grows daily. She must have led a lonely life in her apartment after my father died. I know she often felt frustrated by my sister, her care partner, whose personality was at the opposite end of the spectrum from her own. As time went on, she became increasingly judgemental and critical in her remarks. A sociable person by nature, she must have felt abandoned by friends and neighbours, who may have been alienated by the changes in her personality, and perhaps also repelled by her worsening symptoms.

Struggling with my own unresolved anger, I was of no help at all. I still writhed under the assaults of her tongue. I was afraid to enter her world; so it never entered my mind to ask her what it was like to have Parkinson's. If I had known then what I know now, would I have been more compassionate and less judgemental? Would I have made allowances? Would I have recognized that some of her unacceptable behaviour was due to cognitive change and not to deliberate malice? There is a certain poetic justice in my having what she had, and possibly facing the same cognitive deterioration and the emergence of a shadow side no longer subject to my control.

My mother died in 1990. I remained frozen in resentment until the long retreat of 2003—a retreat I experienced as "grace-filled, healing, providential, blessed, fearsome, and awe-filled." The conductor was Brother Curtis Almquist, Superior of the Society of St. John the Evangelist. His address on forgiveness was particularly powerful. I could feel the tears welling up as he spoke, and I barely got back to my room before they burst forth. My long-cherished resentment against my parents, my unwillingness to forgive, especially my mother, came into sharp and painful focus.

On one of our monthly retreat days at the convent, I was led to reflect that I did not come into the world as a pure and innocent being who was gradually bent out of shape by the perversity, whether wilful or unintentional, of my parents. No, I (like everyone else) came into the world carrying the weight of millennia of human misshapenness, long before my parents, who undoubtedly intended their best for me and brought me up in the only way they knew. Now I recognize that anger and resentment are beside the point. There is nothing to forgive. We are all in this together, and no one is entitled to pass judgement and claim innocence. Now, at last, I can acknowledge that I too not only suffer, but also contribute to the pain and tragedy of human alienation.

God grant that I may not keep this life-giving insight

locked in my intellect. Rather, may it descend from head to heart, and from heart into action.

⁓

It seemed to me, as a child, that I could never measure up to my mother's standards. On the other hand, I was the apple of my father's eye—until I reached puberty. As is the case with many men (as I learned decades after the damage was done), my sudden transformation into a woman was too much for my father to deal with. I experienced his distancing as rejection, and there was no one who could enlighten me. I knew that, in spite of his great admiration for my mother, he despised women in general. I concluded that the only way I could win him back was by being a brilliant student. So I spent my adolescence suppressing my femininity and being at the top of my class. Deep down, I knew these strategies were not working, but I had absorbed my father's values to such an extent that I could not imagine any alternatives.

The one-hundredth birthday celebration for our Sister Constance in February 2003 provided the occasion for healing the relationship with my father. Ever since I entered the Sisterhood in 1957, I had been known and cherished by Sister Constance as "J. Arch. McLeod's daughter." She still talks about how much she admired my father, who was her school inspector when she was headmistress of our school in Regina.

So, searching for a birthday gift that would be unique and pleasurable to Sister Constance, I had the inspiration of making up a booklet with some of my father's poems, and writing a brief introduction. I had never thought much of Dad's poetry, and it must have been decades since I had last looked at the little collection I brought back with me after emptying the apartment when my mother died. But I had kept it.

As I read through the collection, I selected four poems that seemed to reflect most truly my father's personality and outlook on life, and a very different picture of him began to take shape. About one poem in particular I wrote:

> Through his poetry, my father was able to express aspects of his inner life that were not easy for him to reveal otherwise—his playfulness, his humour, his tenderness, his ability to enter into a child's imaginative world, and most of all, his faith.

> A professed agnostic for most of his life, he began, apparently in his eighties, to write poems with a Christian content. In the last poem in this little collection, he expresses wonder at the purposiveness (a favourite word of his) of even the most minute cells, which have a "consciousness" that cannot be ascribed to mere chance. In this poem, he is able to bring together his lifelong scientific worldview and his newfound faith.

My sister Jean used to tell me that, shortly before he died, my father asked her to read him the fifty-third chapter of Isaiah, in which Christians have found a powerful image of Christ's redemptive suffering. When she had finished reading it, he said simply, "He is the Saviour."

Sister Constance's birthday falls on 2 February, the Feast of the Presentation of Christ in the Temple. Some years ago, I wrote a poem in which I used the image of Simeon receiving the Christ Child into his arms to symbolize the healing of my relationship with my father, which at that time I longed for yet continued to resist. The persistence of Sister Constance, a temple-dweller more aged than Anna, in keeping my father's image before me, has enabled a healing long overdue, of which my poem was prophetic.

Nunc Dimittis
(To J. A. M., 1875–1974)

(Father)
As Simeon could not depart
Until the blessed child appeared,
So let me go away and die;
For I have languished long enough,
Locked in the cellar of your mind.
Place your newborn child in my arms
And let me know myself forgiven.
Release me, let me go in peace.

(Daughter)
Across the gulf that separates
Time from eternity, I call:
It's true, I banished you in scorn
And fear, but could not let you die.
So you have raged within my soul
And will not stop till I forgive,
Revoke the sentence that condemned
You to a living death, too long
Locked in the cellar of my mind.
So now I place my newborn child
Within the circle of your arms,
Release you, let you go in peace.
(20 September 1989)

Suggestions for Reflection/Discussion

For Individuals

- Are there relationships I have lost or left behind that I might be able to heal, if not directly, at least in my mind and heart?

For Care Partners and Families

- How can we keep the core of our relationship with the person we care for as his/her capacity is diminishing? Can the changes actually be stepping stones for a new and better relationship?

For Small Groups

- Who are the most important people in our lives? How can we regard and conduct our relationships with them, whether they are dead or alive, in a way that does justice to both them and us?

Intermezzo

In the last months of 2003, as I prepared to leave Maison St-Jean, St-Lambert, and return to St. John's Convent, Toronto, my homes both old and new, I reflected on the continuities and the discontinuities of my life.

The major continuity is the practice of the religious life—the framework of the daily Divine Office and the Eucharist, the meals and recreation times together. The interpersonal relations are more intense in a branch house of four or five Sisters than at the Mother House. Living so closely together, we learn to take seriously St. Paul's advice about not letting the sun go down on our anger. A branch house can provide an education in interpersonal relationships.

There is more speech and less silence in a branch house. Our meals, except for breakfast, are not silent; and more often than not, we have guests at table with us. We go out more. We attend the Eucharist at a different church each Sunday and are amazed at the diversity in styles of worship and music. When one of us goes out to a church to speak, we all go to support with our presence the Sister who is speaking and also the parish.

Much of my work is what I have been doing for years—conducting quiet days, leading workshops on prayer and on hymns, giving homilies, and giving spiritual direction. New experiences have included being a "presence and a listening ear" at the Montreal Diocesan Seminary one day a week, and my activities at the Ignatian Centre. In the first year, I completed the course on Ignatian Spiritual Exercises in Daily Life and, in years two and three, took the course leading to certification as a Prayer Companion.

The totally unforeseen factor, of course, has been the impact of Parkinson's. Externally, except for the need of more rest and the length of time it takes to accomplish tasks, it has not seriously affected my work or recreation. It was in the summer of 2001, a few months before my diagnosis, that I walked from the Anglican Cathedral, located in the heart of downtown Montreal, via the Jacques Cartier Bridge, to our house in St-Lambert. Provided that I get enough rest, I have been able to carry on with the usual household activities and the outside speaking. During these years there has been no noticeable change in my organ playing. I have played services from time to time at two South Shore churches, and daily on the small instrument in our chapel.

The most significant differences are the changes with regard to my values, my interpersonal relationships, and my relationship with God. I have begun to see how much pain in my life has been caused by the belief that my acceptance by others depended on my intelligence, my diligence, and my accomplishments. With this has been a belief that it is a sign of weakness to seek help from others, and to reveal one's emotional difficulties. Healing began when I recognized that I could not carry the burden alone. I began to realize how lonely I had been. I began to discover that I was valued and loved for being myself. My trust in God deepened and my prayer became richer. As I was soon to discover, there were still several important issues that I had not faced; but it was not long before they confronted me and, despite the anguish they caused, became the means of healing and grace.

Suggestions for Reflection/Discussion

For Individuals
- According to my own perception, why am I accepted by others? How may that perception change now?

For Care Partners and Families
- Consider deeply how your family member has influenced your lives. If the influence has been mainly positive, tell her/him. If it has been mainly negative and remains so, will telling her/him change things, or will simply recognizing the truth be all that you need?

For Small Groups
- According to our own perception, why are we accepted by others? Have we checked the reality of that perception?

Coming Home to a Strange Land

Home is where one starts from . . .

We shall not cease from exploration
And the end of all our exploring
Will be to arrive where we started
And know the place for the first time.
(T. S. Eliot, *Four Quartets*)

The story of my life with Parkinson's has been a story of moves. First came the move out of the assistant's office in 1999 into a music "office" at one end of a large multipurpose room. Then a year later came the move to St-Lambert, where I lived for the better part of four years. In January 2004 I moved back to the Mother House on Botham Road in Toronto.

The next moves involved the whole community. In July 2003 we had sold to a developer our property on Botham Road where we had lived for fifty years, and in September of that year celebrated the ground-breaking ceremony for the new convent on Cummer Avenue. By the time I returned to Toronto in the winter of 2004, work was well underway. For financial reasons we chose to move in September 2004 to the building that was to become the new Guest House. Then, early in January 2005, we moved into the beautiful new building that was to be our home.

At my request I had been assigned a room in the Infirmary. I was already receiving such help as assisted showers, change of bed linen, and laundry service; these services would now be available, and others would be added as needed. For me, however, to move into a room in the Infirmary was also a rite of passage—a tangible symbol, and a celebration of having successfully negotiated the transition from middle age to elderhood. Or had I?

When I walked into my Infirmary "suite"—the spacious bedroom with its own two-piece washroom—the words that came spontaneously to me were, "Here will I dwell, for I have a delight therein." And so it has proved, though I gradually realized that it also brought its own temptations. It could easily become my little world, where I could escape the bustle and pressures of a busy household. As an introvert with a head full of projects, I found it all too tempting to busy myself in space that served as bedroom, office, and craft room.

It has taken me a long time to accept the challenges of being old and out of the mainstream of convent life and activity, but by choosing to live in the Infirmary, I opted wholeheartedly for membership in a family within the larger family of the convent household—a family to which every member belongs because of some infirmity of body or mind. It is easy for me to be with those who can carry on a conversation. Spending time with those who are unresponsive or cognitively challenged is another matter. I find this particularly hard because I have been articulate all my life, and have never developed the skills of non-verbal communication. It is a challenge to learn these skills, but the rewards are great.

I had a foretaste of how bonds can be created in other

ways than the spoken word. Sister Madeleine Mary has a very limited ability to communicate verbally, but she can sing the melodies of hymns and songs that were popular in her youth. One evening I came upon two Sisters singing gospel songs, in which Madeleine Mary joined with obvious pleasure as she was able. I stopped and sang with them. As we sang together, I felt that we had succeeded momentarily in easing Madeleine Mary's loneliness and connecting her with the life of our community.

The Infirmary family also includes the staff—a mixture of Jamaican, Philippine, and Chinese women. All of them are kind-hearted and capable. Our relationship with them is shaped by the fact that they shower us, clean up after us when needed, and make sure we get our medications. The result is an easy intimacy, tempered by an appropriate professional reserve.

Along with the moving of bodies, belongings, and furnishings come those inner movements of the Spirit by which, little by little, our lives may be healed and transformed. When I arrived at the convent from St-Lambert, I had much to learn, much to unlearn, and much to be healed. This, to be sure, would be the work of a lifetime; at the time, however, it seemed like a crash course!

I think I expected the transition from Montreal to Toronto to be easy. I would sail in, take up where I left off, and everything would go smoothly and predictably. Of course there had been changes in the convent life, as might be expected in a healthy community. I had not taken into account the extent to which Parkinson's had changed me and the resulting impact it would have on my reintegration into convent life.

At first, I was just plain confused. Many things had stayed the same, but many other details had changed just enough that I could no longer move with the ease and assurance of long familiarity. Then came the discovery that my job as music coordinator had changed too. I was given a rapid tour through a maze of computer files, containing all the records of the music department, and an array of new procedures, none of which had existed four years earlier.

Furthermore, I and the Sister who worked with me in the tiny office space we shared were of very different temperaments. She was a professional violinist who in mid-life was studying piano as a prelude to organ, so that she could in time share with Sister Constance Joanna and me the accompaniment of the choir. I stood in awe of her musical experience, including having played in symphony orchestras. She had never previously studied a keyboard instrument.

One day she played some piano music before a chapel service. Later in the day I told her how much I had appreciated her playing. She said that no one—no one at all—had given her any feedback. Then without warning, she exclaimed with considerable passion, "I *hate* what this disease is doing to you." I was dumbfounded—it was the first time she had expressed concern or given any indication of having the slightest idea of the impact of Parkinson's on me. She added (almost as if she had read my mind), "People think I am all brain, but I do have feelings, too." We exchanged hugs and went our ways.

My difficulties in processing large amounts of information at once, my frustrating slowness, and my need for rest, exercise, and self-care—not to mention the special events and the plethora of meetings during the early months of 2004—meant that it might take me a week to do what I had once been able to accomplish in a day. If anything was added to my usual workload, I had the sense of falling hopelessly behind. I often felt compelled to use time meant for rest or prayer to keep abreast with my perception of the demands of my work. It was not a wise decision, and it established a pattern from which I still struggle to get free.

One particular cause of distress was the decision, made before my return, that an outside organist would not only continue to play at the Sunday Eucharist, but would take on the big occasions—Easter, Pentecost, and more immediately, the Eucharist for Sister Constance's hundredth birthday celebration. I spent much of the last-mentioned service in tears—partly because of the sheer beauty of the music and the eloquence of some of the hymn texts, partly because my singing voice kept failing, but chiefly because I knew deep down that I no longer had the energy to do the preparatory work or the stamina to meet the demands of such an occasion. I came at last to realize that I was in mourning, and that it was right for me to mourn. And so, in the privacy of my room, I let the tears flow freely whenever they welled up.

Since then, I have come to learn that in a chronic, progressive illness, grieving is a process that must be gone through again and again. Each spell of grieving probes, and in time brings insight and healing to, some vulnerable area in one's life.

I learned as well the extent to which stress can worsen symptoms, how they can subside when the stressful situation comes to an end, and in the meantime how they can be relieved by effective medical interventions. During the first several months in Toronto, symptoms began to surface that medication had once controlled, and new symptoms appeared. Insomnia became a problem. A poor night's sleep not only left me physically tired the following day; it increased my anxiety level and my vulnerability to emotional upset. I felt very fragile. The symptoms were close enough to the surface that even a small upset, whether of mood or plans, could cause them to break through.

I learned how crippling anxiety can be, and how easily it can explode into panic. It seemed that for weeks at a time I felt the lurking presence of anxiety, poised and ready to envelop and paralyse me. During a demanding festal season, I was given the additional assignment of liaison between the Sisterhood and the director of the St. James' Singers, one of the choral groups of St. James' Cathedral in downtown Toronto. Our task was to select music for a benefit concert for our building fund. The concert would feature music and texts by members of SSJD. I undertook the assignment in fear and trembling; it was the kind of responsibility that leaves me struggling with self-doubt and in a state close to desperation.

I need not have worried. The concert was magnificent. I heard music I had written sung with the greatest sensitivity and artistry, drawing out depths and nuances I could not have imagined to be there. This experience so moved me that, when it was my turn to give my talk on "The Divine Office—Continuity and Change," I rose to the occasion in a way that took me by surprise. I received a round of hearty applause and many favourable comments as we mingled after the concert was over.

Later that evening, alone in my room, I suddenly realized with a shock of horror that I had completely forgotten about the Parkinson Society conference I was to have attended the previous Saturday. The result for me was confusion and loss of confidence. The least pressure, the slightest deviation in plans or routine, brought on anxiety. There was scarcely a day when I did not have to decide what I would skip—prayer-time, rest, or exercise—just to meet the requirements of the day or my own fatigue. My formal prayer-times were perfunctory, devoid of any warmth or devotion.

Truly the "strange land," to which I was coming home, was within me. That land, at once parched and sodden, crying mutely for healing, was the terrain I was being driven to explore.

Meanwhile, there was the business of getting onto the Ontario Health Insurance Plan and finding new health professionals—a family doctor, a neurologist, a dentist, an audiologist, and a speech-language pathologist. Fortunately, through the Parkinson Society, I was directed to the Movement Disorders Centre of the Toronto Western Hospital, a centre of international repute, and was able to get an appointment with Dr. Susan Fox—just days after my OHIP had become effective.

I was fortunate too in the matter of a family doctor. Our community was looking for a doctor who would make house calls to our Sisters in the Infirmary. Dr. Diana Heath, a practising Anglican, was not only willing but enthusiastic about taking us on. She began to see us before we moved into the new convent.

I decided to wait until September 2004 before joining a support group or an exercise group. I did, however, enrol in the eight-week "Living Well With Parkinson's" program at the North York General Hospital's Seniors Health Centre. Later I joined the North York support group. I kept in touch with the Ontario and national offices of the Parkinson Society. I sold tulips. I attended the World Parkinson's Day celebrations, hosted by the society in the spring of 2005, and the annual general meeting of Parkinson Society Canada. I also attended a twelve-week speech therapy group led by Bonnie Bereskin in her home. Besides the therapy, the course provided time for exchanges of thoughts and experiences about speech difficulties and other aspects of Parkinson's. One member spoke of the spending spree caused by one of her medications, adding that, fortunately for her bank account, she had shopped for her new wardrobe at the Value Village!

Meanwhile, I continued to make new friends and revive old friendships. Moreover, I was blessed by the help and sensitivity of Sisters who understood my situation. Sister Constance Joanna and her assistant, Sister Elizabeth Ann (later to be elected Reverend Mother), even though heavily involved in all aspects of the building program, were unfailing in their support and encouragement. Front-line support came from three Sisters, all of them nurses: Sisters Patricia, Margaret Mary, and (somewhat later) Brenda. Margaret Mary (later to become the Reverend Mother's assistant), having learned much about Parkinson's through Art Lawson's stays at the convent in earlier years, understood my situation without the need of explanations on my part. Her firmness in reminding me to get enough rest has helped me to be disciplined in caring for my legitimate needs.

So it was that by the time we were ready for the big move in January 2005, the convent was no longer a strange land to me, and I was better prepared to face the changes in my health and the changes that awaited all of us in the months that followed.

Suggestions for Reflection/Discussion

For Individuals
- Try to describe the "strange land" you find yourself in. How different is this new life from the "strange land" you were in when you first noticed symptoms of your disease, or the signs of "aging"?

For Care Partners and Families
- In what ways is your "strange land" different from your family member's?

For Small Groups
- What can we learn from the description of the "family" of a religious order?

The Way of Wisdom

O come, O Wisdom from on high
who orders all things mightily;
to us the path of knowledge show
and teach us in her ways to go.
Rejoice! Rejoice! Emmanuel
shall come to you, O Israel.

(9th Century—John Mason Neale, translator)

The wisdom of the Sisters of St. John the Divine, of friends, and of health professionals has helped me in my own quest for wisdom—the practical wisdom that would enable me to reach a deeper level of understanding of issues related to my condition.

Once, while describing to Sister Margaret Mary a particularly helpful session on energy management that I had attended, I said as an afterthought, little knowing how it would change my life: "They were even trying to convince us to use walkers—well, I won't be needing that for long time!" Margaret Mary's reply was prompt and decisive: "You need one NOW!" Being the Convent Clerk of the Works and a woman of action, she paged our maintenance manager and asked him to bring a walker out of storage. This delivered, she hailed one of the cleaning staff and asked her to clean it up for me. Meanwhile she herself made a label with my name and address and affixed it to the walker. Then she gave me a demonstration and admonished me, "Now, you use it."

Use it I did, at first when I felt the need and later when I needed it all the time to steady my gait and prevent falls. I have to admit that I was not thrilled with the prospect. However, I respected Margaret Mary's judgement, for she is a competent and experienced nurse. By this time, too, I had learned that others can sometimes be more objective than myself in assessing my needs.

Soon after I began to use the walker, it was decided that I was no longer to travel by public transport, but to rely on a Sister or the Direct Patient Service to get me to my various appointments. I had been an enthusiastic walker most of my adult life. In 1998 I had celebrated my seventieth birthday by walking downtown from our Botham Road convent, located just north of Highway 401. In 2000, when I was already having Parkinson symptoms without knowing it, I had walked from Christ Church Cathedral, in the heart of downtown Montreal, across the Jacques Cartier Bridge to our house in St-Lambert. Accepting the fact that I was no longer capable of such long-distance walks was not too difficult. What I missed most was the freedom to go exploring the city alone or with a friend, or being able to go by public transport to a friend's house. My disappointment, however, was tempered by the knowledge that I no longer had the energy or the stamina for these excursions.

Using a walker immediately moved me from the able-bodied to the visibly handicapped, with all the stereotypes and misconceptions that this might evoke. On the other hand, using the walker makes it easier for me to converse with strangers, especially if I return their gaze with a friendly smile.

One of the major problems I have had in living with Parkinson's has been time management. I have tried all sorts of schedules and, with luck, have succeeded in keeping to them for a few days. By nature I am more space-oriented than time-oriented. It may well be that I was trying to order time in the same way as I would order space. Small wonder that my little blocks of time would never stay put. If space is like a building, time is like a river. Each has a law and a life of its own.

Perhaps there was an unrecognized reluctance to admit that being an elder is not just being a middle-aged person who happens to be seventy-five. Despite all the evidence to the contrary, I was trying to live as though still in the prime of life. I filled every nook and cranny of the day with work or personal projects, ignoring the need for rest until fatigue forced me to go and lie down. But for the limitations that Parkinson's brought, I might have spent the rest of my days trying to live as though old age was something that happened to other people.

Sue Lawson, who had become a staunch friend, helped me in making the transition from mid-life to elderhood. She proposed three tasks, which I began on my next retreat day:

Grieve for what you are losing;
Learn how to become an elder; and
Map—plan what can be done with the remaining time/energy.

Grieve for what you are losing. The first loss I identified was that as a semi-active Sister, I had moved from the centre to the periphery of community life. I felt out of the loop. I had always been where the action was; now I was a bystander as the herculean task of the double move went on. Sisters my own age were carrying huge responsibilities. But for Parkinson's, I would have been one of them.

Then, of course, there were the limitations imposed by my condition itself. The extreme slowness of movement and thought, the lack of energy and the fatigue, all severely limited what I could accomplish in a day. I seemed to be perpetually behind with daily tasks and long-term projects alike. Minor cognitive changes such as the lack of focus and motivation and the inability to deal with detail were difficult for me and confusing for people who had seen me in my prime. The loss of motor skills and power of concentration kept me from playing most of my organ repertory. Uncertainty in voice production often took the pleasure out of singing.

Knowing that, in a progressive illness, the grieving process must be gone through again and again, I realized that I would need to be willing to stay with each new loss until I was given the peace that comes with acceptance.

Learn how to become an elder. Given all these diminishments, how was I to learn to be an elder? I would need to pray for the grace not only to come to terms with my losses but also to recognize the gifts hidden in them. One such gift is a positive attitude toward my illness; another, a sense of humour that has actually improved; and likewise, an empathy with others with health problems. Sisters often tell me that I am an inspiration to them; if so, I must never forget that this is pure gift. Any attempt of mine to be an inspiration would be self-defeating.

I needed to give myself permission to enjoy life; to build-in times of leisure and enjoyment, to nurture friendships, and have fun, rather than feeling that I must fill every second with something I could justify as useful. Though I could spend a whole day very happily in my room, I needed the social dimension for a balanced life.

Recognizing that my "core gift" is creativity, I felt a strong need to garner up what I felt to be of lasting value in words and music, as my legacy to the community and perhaps beyond. This too would flourish only in a leisurely approach to life. At the same time, I felt a sense of urgency and a need to write and compose while I still had the physical and mental capacity. I would have to unlearn pressuring myself and work in a peaceful, even a contemplative, way. I would need to simplify, prioritize, and be realistic about what I could achieve. Fortunately, both Sister Constance Joanna and her successor as Reverend Mother, Sister Elizabeth Ann, were sympathetic. My workload was substantially reduced in order to give me time for writing and composing.

Map—plan what can be done with the remaining time/energy. A favourite saying of Sue Lawson is, "Parkinson's is a full-time job," to which I reply, "So is life in a convent!" How to integrate these two realities has not been easy. I am learning, little by little, that I have to be committed to change if it is going to happen. That involves being open to be shown—whether by friends, health professionals, or the Holy Spirit—what needs to be changed and how to begin.

The most fruitful approach for me is to identify the activities that are most important to me—and most beneficial—and also those that I routinely forget or postpone until I am too tired. Adequate sleep heads the list. Next comes health care: exercise, a thorough cleaning of teeth, and an afternoon nap. There must also be an important block of time for creative writing or composing and the spiritual duties to which we are committed by our Rule of Life.

I think I have set some priorities of my own, based on the fear and assumption that incapacity or even death may overtake me before I write my book, catalogue my compositions, and edit my poetry. What I need more than anything is a willingness to trust God, who has the final decision to make as to what I can complete and what I must leave behind. The other gift I need is the conviction that what I write is worth sharing. Hopes dashed and promises forgotten, ridicule masked as teasing, contempt for womanhood—all these have left me with a sense of inadequacy, a lack of self-confidence which has hobbled me almost up to the present. It is ironic that it took an illness like Parkinson's to set me free to be myself and therefore to say what I have to say in prose, poetry, and music.

Looking at an illustrated prose-poem I had written during my long retreat in 1999, I could see that I had caught a glimpse of my divided self, and also the way to healing:

Once upon a time

I packaged up my life (1950)
neat, noncommittal, anonymous....
I carried it around with me
wrapped tight,
until I almost forgot
what was inside.

After a while, it seemed to me
that I'd left it behind somewhere,
but I hadn't.

In fact,
one day I discovered
that I had tied it to my back.
My shoulders ached with the burden...
And so it went on year after weary year
until I could carry it no further...
(1950–1999)

Then I heard a voice I had not known saying,
"I took the burden off your back—

I let you put down your load."
"Who are you?" I ask.
"I am the one who bears your griefs
and carries your sorrows."
"Have you really been carrying mine?"
The stranger does not reply, but hands me the package
he has taken from my back.
"Open it!" he says.
I take the box, hesitate—who knows what horrors I'll
find inside.
He smiles—and waits.
So, laboriously, I begin to untie the knots I tied
a lifetime ago.
"Couldn't we just cut the strings?"
No answer—he smiles and waits.

At last, the knots untied, I remove the paper,
open the lid....
"Well," he says, "Do you like what you see?"
"I don't see anything. The box is empty."
Then he hands me a mirror. Do you like what you
see?
I see a woman, vibrant, passionate, in love with life,
yet seasoned with the wisdom of a fifty-year journey.
Yes, I reply. I LIKE WHAT I SEE.

We journey on together.
(Signpost pointing the way to 2000)

It was this woman who was bound up and hidden within me.
Now it was my task to unbind her and let her go free; but this could
happen only if I walked with the One who makes us free indeed.

Suggestions for Reflection/Discussion

For Individuals

- Why do I grieve losing? Have I lost capacities before that I did not grieve fully enough? What do I need to learn about becoming an elder—not an older person, but an elder?

- What does it take me to "rest with each new loss" until there is peace and contentment?

For Care Partners and Families

- What are you grieving the loss of, because of your family member's illness?

- What can you plan, and what can you not plan, because of your concerns for your family member?

- What will help you to "rest with each new loss" until there is peace and contentment?

For Small Groups

- What is the difference between being an older person, a senior, and being an elder?

- What do I need to learn about becoming an elder—not an older person, but an elder? What do others hope for, from their elders?

- Read about indigenous people and their understanding of elders. What can we learn from their understanding?

Bridging the Great Divide

When mind and body wed, there is more joy
in heaven and earth than though they had remained
whole and unsundered from the first creation;
Yet such a union's but a broken toy
when mind recoils, its spotless mirror stained,
While body, widowed, learns its desolation.
(T. A., SSJD)

Late in January 2005, as I was walking along the link connecting the new convent to the Guest House, I glimpsed
my shadow in profile. "I'm developing a real Parkinson stoop,"
I mused. I thought nothing more about it until a week or so
had passed, when my stoop became so obvious that no one
could miss it. My head and neck were pushed forward, and my
trunk was so bent over that I had to twist my head around to
see the face of the person I was talking to. Not surprisingly,
the whole balance of my body was upset. I had several near-
falls, and festination became my preferred way of locomotion,
controlled only by using the walker. The worst feature was a
steady ache in the lower back, increasing and spreading right
up to the neck, brought on by any exertion, and particularly
by upward stretching. In retrospect, I noted that for some
months I had had such aches but only sporadically. The next
development was a pronounced list to port. This could be

embarrassing—when sitting next to a man I did not know, I kept leaning over sideways, almost into his lap!

As these features became more prominent, my balance became more precarious. I had a series of falls, including one that landed me on my forehead and produced a spectacular set of "raccoon's eyes" in rich shades of purple and burgundy. I still fall from time to time. If, for example, I forget myself and make a quick turn, I am likely to end up on the floor. On one occasion, my posterior collided with the rim of a metal waste paper basket on my way down. It left a sickle-shaped bruise that was quite artistic, but the only persons who could admire it were the nurses who give me my shower!

There was no question about it: I needed a physiotherapist right away. Fortunately, help was available right next door, at St. John's Rehab Hospital, founded by us in the 1930s and still connected at the levels of senior management and pastoral care. Through the good offices of Sister Brenda, the Mission Director, I was enabled to begin at once with Araceli Landaburu, the therapist who works with our neurological patients. I was with Araceli for six months, and what an experience it proved to be! I can hardly find words to describe it. Words like "philosophical," "mystical," and "meditative" come to mind, but none of them quite hits the mark. There is a determination, an energy in her that gives no quarter. We worked hard, and mostly in silence. She did not want verbal feedback; instead, she prodded and kneaded deeply, reading my body in a way that reminds me of Psalm 139: " Lord, you have searched me out and known me."

Our work together brought into focus issues I have been struggling with since childhood. After a particularly searching session of physiotherapy, Araceli observed that, to her surprise, the stiffest area in my whole body was my head. "You are all head," she added. She went on to speak of the self-healing properties of the body. This was a moment of insight for me, confirming an idea that had come to me a few days earlier: the extent to which my life is dominated by a body/mind dualism.

By its very nature, a dualism has a tendency to take good versus evil as its model. It assumes that the person is the mind, and the body merely an instrument for carrying out what the mind ordains. In Parkinson's, when the slow and unresponsive body doesn't leap to fulfil the mind's every whim—and be quick about it—the lively and agile mind becomes impatient and berates the body for its slowness, clumsiness, and general ineptitude. So as I learn to respect my body's pace and needs, and to delight in my body's grace, a great healing will result and a tiny portion of the world will have been reclaimed for wholeness, wisdom, and sanity.

As I began to learn this new way of experiencing my body, Araceli was ready with another life-changing insight. One day she said in fun, but with serious intent, "You're the first person with Parkinson's whom I've ever had to slow down." I was surprised and a little miffed. After all, bradykinesia (slowness), along with rigidity, had been my first symptom to emerge, and had remained the most prominent.

On further reflection, I realized that she was right. Slow as I am, I kept pushing myself to move faster. I have always been somewhat slow physically and quick mentally. This in itself has set up a long-standing source of tension. I can also catch echoes of various voices from the past, like my mother's ("Hurry up, Thelma-Anne. Don't dawdle!") and many others that I cannot remember. Once again through Parkinson's, I was given the opportunity for insight and healing.

It dawned on me that much of my fatigue comes from pushing myself instead of listening to my body. As I become more adept in picking up my body's signals, I realize that this sets me free to choose between the old way and the new. When I revert to the old way, anxiety, impatience, and a sense of drivenness emerge at once. It is no surprise that back pain, balance problems, festination, and fatigue soon follow.

All this has implications for a life of prayer. It is hard to pray when the mind is trying to pressure the body to keep up with its own giddy pace. The mind is so busy with its incessant chatter that it cannot hear other voices—those of the body, of people around them, and the still, small voice of God. But there are moments of stillness. One morning, I was not just thinking incessantly; I was talking aloud in an unending commentary on what I was doing until, when stopping for breath, I heard the inner voice say, "Will you please leave some space for Me."

The voice of the body is a "sound of sheer silence" (cf. the prophet Elijah's encounter with God, 1 Kings 19:12), which enables attentiveness to God. Sometimes we experience this silence while walking, when the focus of attention shifts from the inner monologue to the silence and slowness of the body. This too brings a contemplative stillness, as the mind adopts the silent, slow pace of my body. Walking meditation is based on this experience. One day, when walking along the corridor, I actually felt my impatience, my effort to make my body go as fast as my mind dictated, "Stop that," I said to myself. "You don't need it. Get the feel of how your legs are moving and let them set the pace." At once the pressure and anxiety disappeared.

This intentional slowing down benefits every aspect of life. We are not aware of the ways we push ourselves until someone tells us. One day Araceli said to me, "You even festinate when you talk!" I thought I was talking at an average speed, but immediately switched to what I thought was a very deliberate pace. "Is that any better?" I asked. "You're still talking very fast. Your tongue can't keep up with your mind." Caught again!

The next time I played a hymn, I caught myself racing along and getting more and more anxious as wrong notes proliferated. I deliberately slowed down, and immediately the anxiety melted away. I enjoyed the music and the feeling that I was in charge instead of being swept away by a force I could not control. I was getting a taste of a new way of living, based on a peaceful attentiveness and enjoyment. Araceli has taught me some practical ways: one is to walk "head over heels"; another is to feel the ground you are walking on with every muscle in your feet. Because of the total attention given to our silent body, we are able to become deeply silent within, and in that silence we may well receive what can only come as a gift when we are ready to receive it—the experienced presence of God.

In July 2003 I was already becoming aware of the connection between slowness and inner stillness but lacked the motivation to live what I had written:

I am learning a new discipline—writing legibly. My thoughts crowd at the tip of my pen and jostle each other to get out onto the page. Some of them simply evaporate into silence. It has been said, "Before speaking, consider whether it is an improvement upon silence." Perhaps the same principle applies to writing. I look at the clean white page and ask myself, "Will what I write be an improvement?" Perhaps so, perhaps not. I hope it will be a wholesome discipline.

Why am I doing this? In practical terms, I want to be able to read what I write. I also want to clothe my thoughts in a vesture more pleasing to the eye than my usual cramped, micrographic scratches. More importantly, I want to slow down my thoughts, to prune, to simplify. This is an exercise in de-cluttering, in simplicity, and holy poverty. Instead of racing ahead, I find myself pausing, waiting in silence for the next thought to form, considering what I really want to say and how to say it.

Why am I doing this? To bring my rapacious mind into harmony with my slowed down brain. To open myself to the peace that—quite literally—passes understanding. To think and write contemplatively, and to let this contemplative peace flow into my hurried and harried life. To open myself to wisdom, to still my inward chatter so as to hear the silent speech of God. To find, in my slowness, not frustration but grace.

As I explore the implications and meaning of these reflections, there emerges a comprehensive healing pattern for living well. The mind/body dualism locks us into a rigid, either/or pattern that sets up a conflict that is, in fact, not there. Everything is either good or bad. Mind is good; therefore body is bad. This has implications for prayer. When a dualistic pattern prevails, our prayers tend to become wordy and intellectualized. Our mind is as busy as ever. We pay scant attention to the body, which is seen as an impediment to prayer. Since the body and its impulses are understood to be, if not downright evil, at best a nuisance, and at worst, a temptation that lures us away from union with God, we can use a tremendous amount of energy trying to drive out the evil impulses of the body.

The discipline of inner silence and the recurring rhythms of the monastic timetable give shape, proportion, and durability to my life. There is a life-giving strength in knowing that I am not going through life alone, but in company with a community of women committed to the lifelong discipline of loving God and one another. In T. S. Eliot's profound image, we open ourselves to learn how to "move in measure, like a dancer" (T. S. Eliot, *The Complete Poems and Plays*. New York: Harcourt, Brace and Company, 1952, p. 142). Meanwhile, we endure the painful tension between our wilfulness and the divinely established parameters of human life. This deliberate adjusting of tempo between mind and body, this patient endurance of the tension between them, is the way of wisdom, healing, and peace.

Suggestions for Reflection/Discussion

For Individuals

- How do my head and body collide? How can I help them live in harmony?

For Care Partners and Families

- How do my mind and body collide? What can I do to reduce the force of that collision?

- How do I slow down when I'm so busy?

For Small Groups

- Where does the body/mind dualism come from that we find so ingrained? What are the ways others have found to help them live in harmony? What can I do to live in harmony?

A Whiff of Tribulation

A good part of the tribulations of patients
(and their physicians)
comes from unreal attempts to transcend the
possible,
to deny its limits, and to seek the impossible:
accommodation is more laborious and less exalted,
and consists, in effect, of a painstaking exploration
of the full range of the real and the possible.
(Oliver Sacks, *Awakenings*)

Let the righteous smite me in friendly rebuke
(Psalm 141:5a, *The Book of Alternative Services*)

In his profound and insightful book, *Awakenings*, Oliver Sacks (First Perennial Library, 1990) speaks of the post-encephalitic patients he treated with the then-new drug levodopa as going through three phases. First came *awakening*, quite literally in the case of most of these people, who had existed in a state of inertness for as long as twenty years. The awakenings were spectacular, marked by the disappearance of the acute Parkinsonian symptoms that had plagued them, and a tremendous outburst of energy and euphoria. The hopes raised by this experience were sooner or later dashed with the onset of even more bizarre symptoms than before. Finally, with perseverance and tremendous courage, the patients won through to a state that was neither illness nor health, but a viable accommodation to the realities of their lives.

Sacks suggests that people with "ordinary Parkinson's" may encounter this sequence of events in a much milder form. The "dopamine honeymoon" that many experience to some degree corresponds with the awakening. The tribulations take various forms with degrees of intensity; at the very least they take the bloom off the feeling of wellness that the medication produced at the outset. Accommodation means an acceptance of the fact that one has changed irrevocably, and a willingness to order one's life accordingly, finding realistic, wise, and creative ways and means to cope with what is now recognized as the norm. And since Parkinson's, unlike post-encephalitic Parkinsonism, is a progressive condition, the threefold pattern of awakening, tribulation, and accommodation may be repeated many times, each cycle probing more deeply and calling for new understandings.

I had pondered Sacks's words about accommodation for a couple of years or more, but its practical implications were lost on me. I recognized on an intellectual level that such an acceptance of a new reality was called for, but failed to make a connection between this insight and my day-to-day living. A friend can often give one a glimpse of the obvious that one has overlooked. One day Sister Sue, my colleague in the music department, began a conversation in which she remarked that I was still not respecting my limitations, but was trying to work as I could before I had Parkinson's. She went on to explain how accepting limitations related to the threefold vows we profess. The limits on what could be accomplished in a day were something I could try to ignore or fight against; or they could be a God-given opportunity to live out my vow of poverty. Since my illness and the limitations it imposed were permitted (not "sent") by God, to accept them was a form of obedience.

I was well aware that God had made my condition a means of grace, but I had never thought of my response in terms of our threefold vows. Sue had mentioned poverty and obedience. She did not mention chastity, but I reflected that my attachment to my old self and its values was a breach of chastity in the sense that I had put them first in my life, however fervently I wrote about my love for God. I had already felt a dissonance between what I wrote and how I lived, but it was Sue's "friendly rebuke" that brought it into focus.

This sent me back to read what Oliver Sacks might have to say about accepting limitations and found that he considered this to be the essence of "accommodation." He wrote:

> It is a characteristic of many neurologists (and patients) that they mistake intransigence for strength, and plant themselves like Canutes before the advancing seas of trouble, *defying* their advance by the strength of their will ... one takes arms by becoming a mariner in the seas of oneself. "Tribulation" was about trouble and storm; "Accommodation" is concerned with weathering the storm. (p. 265)

Sacks goes on to say, "A good part of the tribulations of patients (and their physicians) comes from unreal attempts to transcend the possible, to deny its limits, and to seek the impossible." Accommodation has to do with real life in the here-and-now and consists, Sacks suggests, of a painstaking exploration of the full range of the real and the possible.

⚘

It is notorious that patients on levodopa therapy will sooner or later develop the symptoms that Sacks calls tribulations.

These may range from mild to severe. Typically people with Parkinson's will experience a reduced ability to tolerate strain in whatever form, and a need for rest and ease and an adequate night's sleep. Impediment of movement can bring on acute stress. Acceptance of new limitations and the ability to adapt to them with creative and realistic solutions such as rest, care, and ingenuity, are needed by all patients on levodopa therapy.

This challenged me. I have had no lack of ingenuity; but until now, rest and self-care have ranked low on my priorities.

By the latter part of 2004 and the first few months of 2005, I felt that I was entering a new phase. Symptoms that had been dealt with by adjustments in medication returned, and new ones appeared. No doubt the convent move and resettlement contributed, as did my all-too-familiar depression and anxiety; but there was an intensity, a weird quality, that was new to me.

The most troubling and debilitating side-effects were insomnia and, hand in hand with it, for the first time a kind of obsessive-compulsive pattern of behaviour. Typically, at about 2:00 A.M. I had the sense of being ejected from my bed, to spend the next two or three hours reorganizing drawers, clothes closet, and whatever else might come to my attention. The result was, invariably, the loss of several hours of sleep and a weariness that sapped my energy and spoiled my mood the next day.

The climax came one morning when the situation went quite out of control. Within the space of perhaps fifteen minutes, I was driven from one activity to another (including prayer) and was totally unable to stop. It left me in a state of extreme exhaustion. When I described this incident to my neurologist, she attributed it to too much dopamine in my brain. She reduced my daily quota of Sinemet CR by one pill, and tranquillity was restored. When I saw my neurologist again six months later and described this behaviour pattern, which had cropped up again, she said that it had a name: *punding* (from a Norwegian word that, she said with a slightly embarrassed laugh, means "blockhead")!

I felt that my spiritual life was becoming increasingly barren, and that I was actually choosing to give into this strange routine in order to avoid prayer. Suzanne Lawson set me straight. "[Punding] plagued Art—and me!—for many years," she wrote, and went on to assure me that it was not a matter of will, and that I need not worry about lost prayer-time. "The disease itself makes you fuss, be wakeful, and overactive at night. It does not at that time allow you to be quiet and prayerful. It cannot be changed simply by an act of will." My spiritual director, Virginia Varley, CSJ, confirmed this with her usual robust common sense, suggesting that I talk to God while punding, and reminding me that creativity is a form of prayer.

At the same time, there is an element of choice. There are times when I feel the punding coming on, and can roll over and go back to sleep before it gets a grip on me. However, it is ready to pounce on me the minute I get up. There is a fascination about it that is almost irresistible. It feeds on my distractibility and on my insistence on keeping several projects going at the same time. What begins as an intention to tidy one drawer—"This will only take a few minutes"—may end up in several hours of tidying and a corresponding loss of sleep. The only thing that will stop me is the fact that it is time for breakfast. So I throw myself into my clothes—never mind washing—wolf down my breakfast and, if I'm lucky, fly into chapel as the Angelus is being rung.

As I tried to understand what hidden motives might be giving such energy to what I recognized as a destructive behaviour, I began to see that unhealed wounds from childhood played an important part. The fact that I always punded with the door to my room shut suggested secrecy, self-protectiveness, and even guilt and shame. It went back to childhood, and particularly adolescence, when I protected myself and those interests that were most likely to be misunderstood or ridiculed. But punding with the door shut simply intensified my secretive behaviour. To survive, I adopted the role of a good and compliant daughter while developing a pattern of secretiveness, coupled with rebellious behaviour.

In time, my neurologist referred me to a neuropsychiatrist who had made a study of punding. He wrote me a prescription that would help me sleep better and give me some control over the punding.

There are no magic bullets. There is the helpful medication, there is my freedom of choice, and there is the grace of God. Each time I awake at night and have to go to the washroom, I have the choice of going right back to bed, or of finding a fascinating bit of tidying that will keep me busy until my usual waking up time—and leave me exhausted and sore-backed for the rest of the day. One would think that the knowledge of how miserable I'd feel would be a deterrent, but that's not how compulsive-obsessive behaviour works. The other time when I am particularly vulnerable is when I first get up. If I opt for the punding, prayer-time and exercise go down the drain, and I risk being late for chapel.

This is where grace comes in. Grace, like medication, is not a magic bullet. It leaves us free; indeed, it challenges us to make a choice that is life-giving rather than destructive. So every time the temptation comes, the grace is offered. In other words, it is a moment of intimacy between oneself and one's Creator. If accepted, it increases our freedom; if rejected, our decision binds us more firmly to our addiction. Since God's will for us is our freedom, our acceptance of the grace offered signifies our return to a relationship that, on God's part, was never broken. This is true even if one feels remote from God. If, on the other hand, we go blithely ahead, God does not give up on us, but waits to offer the same grace the next time. Continual refusal results in a progressive loss of freedom, but this is our choice, not God's will.

This insight brought an end to the sense of alienation that had resulted in my *feeling* there was no point in seeking a God who had turned away in disgust and left me to my own devices. All this takes place in the depths of our being. It is right and proper that we use our reason as far as it will take us, but the real healing begins when we can trust God enough to accept the gift of intimacy that God wills to bestow when we are ready to receive it.

Oliver Sacks has an interesting suggestion about the essence of Parkinsonism in all its forms. This is the tension between slow (bradykinesia) and fast (festination). In each, the outside and inside mirror each other. "Slow" includes movement, slowness of thought, apathy, loss of executive function (the ability to plan and carry though a project), immobility, inertia, freezing, and depression. "Fast" includes rapid movement, including the fast, tiny steps that tend to accelerate, compromising balance and making falls almost inevitable; also an inner sense of being driven, anxiety, and panic. The two states alternate, and eventually coalesce into a stalemate. A post-encephalitic patient of Sacks called the phenomenon "the goad and the halter" (*Awakenings*, p. 7).

This explanation helped me understand in a new way the long struggle over my impatience with my slowness and my frustration at being always behind. The reality of my situation was that my body had indeed slowed down, but my brain was still going full tilt, and was frustrated that the rest of me could not keep up.

Undoubtedly, the fear of losing initiative and the prospect of all-round incapacity have contributed to my sense of urgency. I want to complete this present project, to compose music, and to catalogue what I have written over a period of half a century and to make available the poetry I have written—before it is too late. And what has been lacking, and has now been restored, is the sense that God will enable me to accomplish all this; if not, then I must die content with what I was permitted to accomplish and leave the rest in God's hands.

Sacks has observed that his patients' acceptance of the truth about their situation stimulates the development of extraordinary inventiveness, resourcefulness, and courage. "Some Parkinsonian patients ... become astute and expert navigators, steering themselves through seas of trouble which would cause less expert patients to founder on the spot" (p. 270). Still, there is a loss of initiative that increases with the progression of the disease. Some basic human needs must be met if the patient is to flourish. Sacks specifies "the establishment of proper relations with the world and—in par-ticular—with other human beings, or *one* other human being" (p. 272) as the one thing needful.

Beyond all medication and other kinds of treatment, Sacks believes, is the power of love. This love is expressed in many ways, and not the least in the care partner's commitment to find new ways of stimulating, and thus including, the patient as a person, a member of the human family. "The essential thing," writes Sacks, "is feeling *at home* in the world, knowing in the depths of one's being that one has a real place in the home of the world." And again, he expresses his belief that "love is the *alpha* and *omega* of being, and that the work of healing, of rendering whole is, first and last, the business of love" (p. 273).

Patients, for their part, having given up false hopes and made their accommodation to the realities of their situation, "come to rest" (in Sir Thomas Browne's beautiful words, quoted by Sacks) "in the bosom of their causes." This "coming to rest" is not passive. It means accepting one's limits and then using experience and ingenuity to solve specific problems. It also means sharing with others what we have learned.

Parkinson's, like other slowly progressive chronic illnesses, provides opportunities to make mistakes and to learn from them; to recognize and accept one's frailties and foibles (and those of others) and above all, to know oneself to be loved by God and by the important people in one's life. I have been blessed by deep and nourishing friendships, and by my vocation to the Sisterhood of St. John the Divine, a community committed to "bear one another's burdens, and [so] ... fulfil the law of Christ" (Galatians 6:2).

Suggestions for Reflection/Discussion

For Individuals
- Before the onset of my disease, when in my life have I gone through the cycle of awakening, tribulation, and accommodation? What can I learn from that past experience to help me now?

- If you are interested in understanding more about the discovery of levodopa, read Sacks's book *Awakenings*, or rent the film.

For Care Partners and Families
- How can we better help our family member feel really "at home" in the world?

- How do we express our love, beyond "doing things"?

For Small Groups
- In our congregation, how do we help people with various illnesses—physical, mental, and emotional—feel "at home" in the world of our faith community? And how do we push them out, make them feel very different?

The Struggle and the Stripping

O God
I know that if I do not love thee
with all my mind, with all my soul
and with all my strength,
I shall love something else
with all my heart and mind and soul and strength.
Grant that putting thee first in all my lovings
I may be liberated from all lesser loves and loyalties,
and have thee as my first love,
my chiefest good
and my final joy.

"You are facing death." These words, spoken by Eric Jensen, SJ, the conductor of my eight-day retreat at Loyola House in 2004, were not easy to hear; yet as a woman in her late seventies, I had every reason to heed them. Moreover, I needed to learn the way of dispossession, for to paraphrase the words of Job in the book of the Bible bearing his name, we bring nothing with us into the world and so we cannot take anything we regard as ours with us when we leave. Indeed, having lost everything, Job begins by saying all the pious things; but he soon moves beyond this to express his anger at God, insisting on his own innocence. I have noticed the same pattern in myself. Up to a point, I was saying the right things and was sure I meant them. Inevitably the anger and frustration broke through. Pious generalities gave way to honest expressions of fear, frustration, and anger.

"Stripping" can be understood in different ways. There is the gradual stripping away that comes with advancing age, and the sudden loss of everything in a natural disaster or crippling highway accident. There is also the voluntary stripping of those who seek a simpler lifestyle, as a protest against the prevailing obsession with acquiring more and more belongings. The vow of poverty taken by people in religious orders is an example of stripping in order to make room for Christ and to follow him in singleness of heart. "Struggle" has both positive and negative aspects. We may struggle against the stripping out of fear of losing our identity, or we may struggle to embrace the stripping, in the confidence that it will enable us to follow Jesus, who lived a simple lifestyle.

Divesting oneself of possessions takes courage and perseverance; what we are unwilling to part with may be an indication of what we are attached to. On the other hand, we may in an overzealous moment throw out things that were important to keep. However, the time will come when we have neither the focus nor the energy for this work. When I sorted my mother's papers after her death, I found them to be in perfect order up to a certain date; after that, chaos reigned. Even now, I find it increasingly difficult to keep my own papers in order.

But the way of dispossession goes much deeper than disposing of material things. There are the lifelong habits and attitudes that make life so difficult, the "emotional programs for happiness" that Thomas Keating describes—ways of protecting ourselves and coping with life that are so ingrained that it is virtually impossible to modify, let alone dislodge them (Thomas Keating, interviewed in *Spirituality & Health*, New York: October 2003, pp. 39–41).

As well, there are activities and interests that, for lack of energy and focus, we can no longer enjoy. I can no longer walk

for miles at a time or play long and complex organ compositions. I cannot work at the computer for hours on end. These
are diminishments that I can learn from and adapt to. More
challenging is the slowness of mind and body that hinders
my getting through the amount of work that I want to accomplish in a single day.

So though I still resist the stripping, I am coming to realize
that it brings blessings. I think back to Teilhard's "passivities
of diminishment," seen as opportunities sent by God to pre-
pare us for death. Whatever the realities of the fall from primal
innocence and pristine health which our myths of creation and
fall portray, at some point spiritual maturity requires that we
recognize that the time will come for each of us to accept the
fact that we will not recover lost gifts and powers in life as we
know it. Nor can we blame chance or evil spirits. The psalmist
strikes a chord deep within us in addressing God as the One
who "like a moth" eats away "all that is dear to us" (Psalm 39:
12, *The Book of Alternative Services*).

To assent to the stripping, to embrace the discipline of mind
and heart needed to cooperate with the grace contained in our
diminishment, is painful to contemplate, difficult to begin, and
impossible (without grace) to sustain. It commits us to learn, a
little at a time and with many backslidings, to accept as from
God's hands, the stripping away of all that is dear—our health,
our independence, our cognitive powers, our illusions of virtue
and competence—in order that at last we know ourselves as finite
beings.

However glorious our eternal destiny, it has been ordained
by God that only through the experience and the acceptance
of our finite state do we gain the mature wisdom, the compassion toward self and others, without which we would be quite
incapable of savouring the joy of heaven.

In the *Four Quartets* by T. S. Eliot there is a memorable

passage about an encounter between the poet and a mysterious yet familiar *alter ego*, who speaks of the stripping away of illusions that advancing years bring to us:

> Let me disclose the gifts reserved for age
> To set a crown upon your lifetime's effort.
> First, the cold friction of expiring sense
> Without enchantment, offering no promise
> But bitter tastelessness of shadow fruit
> As body and soul begin to fall asunder.
> Second, the conscious impotence of rage
> At human folly, and the laceration
> Of laughter at what ceases to amuse.
> And last, the rending pain of re-enactment
> Of all that you have done, and been; the shame
> Of motives late revealed, and the awareness
> Of things ill done and done to others' harm
> Which once you took for exercise of virtue....

The mysterious companion concludes:

> From wrong to wrong the exasperated spirit
> Proceeds, unless restored by that refining fire
> Where you must move in measure, like a dancer.

As I look back on my life I can identify many "things ill done," which at the time I certainly "took for exercise of virtue." I recall several occasions when I took advantage of my position as acting guest mistress to vent my anger on some guests whom I found too demanding or too dependent. Decades later, I tried to find one of these people, in the hope of being able in some way to make amends. I wrote to a priest who was in the guest wing at the time and who, quite justly, called me to account for my inhospitality while I stood by in sullen silence. The priest had completely forgotten the incident and her part in it, nor could she recollect the woman's name. Nevertheless, she wrote a beautiful letter about her own failures to show love and forbearance, and God's readiness to forgive. Having done what I could to make amends, I felt that I had indeed been forgiven. A sense of peace and contentment took the place of the anguish I had experienced as I faced the truth about my behaviour.

In addition to the stripping that advancing years bring, the impact of a chronic, progressive illness forces one to recognize that, like it or not, the stripping has begun in earnest. Our condition challenges us to decide whether to cling to the illusion that life can (or at least should) go on as usual, or to embrace the stripping as a sacrament of God's love. Paradoxically, to assent to the stripping is a choice for life; refusing leads to exhaustion and the spiritual deadness of living with illusion instead of being grounded in truth.

This is not meant to convey the idea that one can, or should, accept the stripping without a struggle and without grieving. Mental and spiritual health require that we face our anger and grief. Only then can we let them go. It took a face-to-face meeting with God for Job to accept his losses and admit that he was holding onto an assumption that his eminence and good deeds protected him from loss: "Therefore I have uttered what I did not understand ... I had heard of you by the hearing of the ear, but now my eye sees you; therefore I despise myself, and repent, in dust and ashes" (Job 42:3b, 5–6).

For me, it has been, and still is, a long journey, a path strewn with abandoned daily timetables and other futile attempts at control, doomed to failure because I insisted on setting unrealistic goals and trying to cram each day full of projects. It took a long time for me to admit even to myself, *that in my determination to run my own life, I was withholding the very thing required of me—my willing assent to the stripping in God's time and way.*

A poem I wrote sometime after my diagnosis shows how, in the struggle to retain control, we raise a barrier of our own making that renders prayer virtually impossible.

Though the outward frame decay
night by night, day by day,
though the stricken brain dissolve
all ambition, all resolve;
though the vital strength decline
through no fault or wish of mine,
far below my conscious thought,
giving what I never sought,
you are there
stripping bare.

Why do I resist your care,
why resist your call to share
in your pain,
never to return again
to the confidence and pride
that have been my lifelong guide
though they lied,
failed and died,
left me with an emptiness
where lies hidden your caress—
my blessedness.

Yet I dread the blessed hour
of surrender—shrink and cower,
turn and run,
seek to shun

light from your effulgent sun
blazing , burning, deep within,
healing hurt, erasing sin,
saying, "Child, I love you still,
well or ill.
Though you still hide from my face,
I sustain you with my grace—
and always will."

In June 2005, when after a two-week holiday I resumed my physiotherapy sessions with Araceli, my stooped posture and hollow chest betrayed the fact that I had reneged on my daily exercise sessions. Araceli reminded me that as "the progression of Parkinson's is *relentless,* so the fight against it must go on every day." She also pointed out that my brain needs all the oxygen it can get to function adequately and noted that my lung capacity had already been diminished by my poor posture.

That word *relentless* threw me into a state of shock. I felt as if I was standing on the edge of a precipice and looking down into an abyss. It was an experience similar to my initial "claiming" of Parkinson's, but at a deeper level. In my determination to be cheerful and positive, I had perhaps not given the dark side of my condition its due recognition. The main issue, however, was my divided soul, a desire for God thwarted by the resistance of what St. Paul called the "old" humanity, determined to control its own destiny.

In my imagination, I saw what appeared to be a flimsy, porous garbage bag, filled with decaying matter of various kinds. I took it to be an image of my "natural" self, entrenched and unwilling to venture beyond what I could control. Although

I would have denied it, I was living as though grace was mine to do what I wanted with it. Meanwhile, the progression of Parkinson's was making a mockery of my efforts to control my life, my strategy of giving God a token allegiance while following my own desires.

With this insight I thought my troubles were over; it seemed to me that the bag of filth was rolling down into the abyss that lay under Golgotha, but I was not going with it. I found that I could pray again. My daily activities, which had resisted my efforts at time management, seemed to flow into each other in a way that was at once ordered and flexible. Even the punding was becoming manageable.

Within a day or two, I was brought back to reality. My obsessive-compulsive drive seemed to attach itself to every-thing I did—everything I wanted to do for my own pleasure: writing, tidying my room, sewing. At the same time, I had such an aversion to what I knew was best for me—resting in the early afternoon, getting to bed at a decent time, prayer and spiritual reading, cleaning my teeth, exercising and walk-ing—that I omitted them one by one.

The only thing that got me out of this morass was a new gift from God—the realization that God was with me, afflicted in my affliction—a loving and affirming Presence that enabled me to live in relative peace with the inner turmoil and the out-ward confusion. I acknowledged what I had long suspected: that it was my fearing the cost of following Christ that was the driving force behind my effort to crowd every moment with work or hobbies—anything to avoid the moment of unmistak-able divine calling that, if responded to, might lead me, like Peter, to a place I had no wish to go.

Now at last I was experiencing stripping as a gift and a way to healing. I had encountered a situation that I could not fix. I was *living* what had been mere rhetoric for me—that I could not claim to be a follower of Christ and then go my own way as though his teaching and, still more, his passion were irrelevant. I knew that I would not be transformed overnight. There would be both progress and backsliding. The tug of war between myself-in-Christ and myself-on-my-own would go on until I drew my last breath.

And that brings me back to Father Jensen's words. Yes, I am facing death, but I am also embracing life. By the grace of God I can, here and now, accept aging and the progression of Parkinson's as part of the stripping that prepares me for that final stripping of life itself that awaits us all. Meanwhile, the struggle and the stripping continue in tension with each other. There remains much to learn and much to unlearn—and no guarantee that the work will be fully accomplished in this life. As for the life to come, I rest in the hope that those who have died in Christ experience "continual growth in God's love and service."

Suggestions for Reflection/Discussion

For Individuals
- Stripping is a "gift and a way to healing." What has been very difficult to strip from my vision of myself? Where am I on the continuum between stripping and desperately clinging?

For Care Partners and Families
- How have we observed our family member's struggles in "stripping" as a way to healing? What stripping have we ourselves had to do? Have we grieved what we have stripped, and then moved to acceptance? Or are we still somewhere en route?

For Small Groups

- Where in our lives have we experienced this healthy stripping that Sister Thelma-Anne refers to? What needs to be stripped but is being fought against?

A Taste of Resurrection

And now in age I bud again.
After so many deaths I live and write;
I once more smell the dew and rain,
And relish versing: O, my only Light,
It cannot be
That I am he
On whom Thy tempests fell all night.
(From "The Flower" by George Herbert)

It has been said, "Experience must be processed until it becomes meaning." As I have been writing and living this story, I have found that patterns emerge, repeat themselves, and change subtly with each repetition. As I look back over these five years, a core issue for me has been to recognize the body as an equal partner with the intellect, and to move this insight from theory to practice. It is an ongoing work that will require a generous and active co-operation with the grace given moment by moment.

At the time of my diagnosis I had no experience and no idea of what it was like to live with a chronic, progressive illness. I could not even imagine how I might change, and how my circumstances might change, as Parkinson's progressed. Once

I had begun to take Sinemet, I was buoyed by the hope that, for the present at least, all would be well. Of course, it was not long before I had to take a more realistic view. However, I was still able to carry on with my life and work, provided that I took adequate rest.

This phase did not last long. Losses, such as the unreliability of my singing voice, and mild cognitive changes that seemed to point to more drastic losses later on, brought me face to face with the reality of diminishment and increasing incapacity. I was able to deal with this up to a point, and my reading of Teilhard de Chardin helped me integrate these losses with my faith and prayer life. In time, however, as new symptoms developed, a subtle pessimism began to lurk beneath the buoyant spirit I had been able to maintain. Deterioration of my organ technique, due partly to loss of fine motor control and partly to my slowness in processing information, seemed to threaten something that had been central in my life and vital to my identity.

The onset of punding moved me into a new dimension of experience. Once it had gained a foothold, it began to crowd out not only activities and interests but the obligations prescribed by our Rule of Life. Even prayer seemed like dust and ashes compared with the illusion of independence that accompanied the punding. As months passed, my aversion to prayer-times grew stronger, and even my faith began to waver. Finally, by the grace of God I recognized the gravity of my situation. In grasping for freedom I had lost it. I was in the clutches of an addiction that had the potential to suck out the substance of my life and faith while preserving the empty forms.

As so often happens, help came from an unsought source. I happened to read an interview with Thomas Keating in a three-year-old issue of *Spirituality &Health: The Soul/Body*

Connection, which turned up on our magazine rack. He talked about centering prayer as a means of healing, a basic concept in Keating's writings on prayer, as I have mentioned earlier in the book. The false self is the one we develop in response to the demands of even the best of parents, who have developed false selves of their own. The true self is the inherently good creation of God.

The false self "grows out of the need for happiness—translated as pleasure or gratification of the instinctual needs of an infant, such as security, approval, power, or control" ("A Simple Prayer, A Profound Freedom," in *Spirituality & Health*, October 2003, p. 40 ff.). Not knowing where true affirmation is to be found, we seek gratification, but we seek it in the wrong places, and our need becomes a craving. The whole vicious circle—desire, frustration, discouragement, or desire and gratification—is repeated over and over again. Our futile search for happiness leads into addiction.

I had both practised and taught centering prayer for years, but had never come across any mention of the connection between the false self and addiction. (And of course it never occurred to me that I might have an addiction.) Healing through centering prayer comes from the inner silence that enables us to receive the gift of knowing God's own motherly presence within us.

In the meantime, my unwillingness to accept help, another expression of my prideful independence, was being challenged, often in the simple, day-to-day interaction with others. The following scenario recorded in my journal illustrates the way the Holy Spirit enabled me to move beyond my fixation on protecting my independence.

A certain member of the Infirmary staff seems determined to fuss over me whether I want to be fussed over or not. One chilly day I go to get my coat off the rack. Maria leaps forward and not only takes it from the rack—she puts it on me, scarf, hat and all, and insists on buttoning up the coat—all of which I am quite capable of doing and would rather do for myself. So out comes my little harangue about maintaining independence as long as possible. Maria simply replies, "I want to help you." Next time: Maria helps me into my coat, smiling (methinks) a bit triumphantly. If she is expecting a repeat of my earlier performance, she is in for a surprise. This time, I smile back (rather triumphantly myself) and thank her.

Reflection on this incident led me to find in it an experience of resurrection. No doubt I was quite capable of putting my coat on, but was this insistence on going it alone Christ-like? Jesus *humbled* himself, putting himself into our hands, at our mercy. Could I then refuse the well-intended, if excessive, help offered by one of the Infirmary staff who was trying to serve the Christ in me. I could take this still further. When I bridle at being helped, insisting on my own independence, am I letting the courteous and accepting Christ in me be Christ? Am I ministering to the sorrowing Christ in me, who suffers because of my harsh expectations and false values, to the bound Christ in me who longs to be free to set me free?

Here are some more "tastes of resurrection"—experiences of life out of death, each bearing for me the signature of the risen Christ. It was the amazing improvement in my posture that gave me the first experience of renewed life. Besides improved posture and renewed energy, the breathing techniques

I learned enabled me to sing with a better tone and greater endurance. As a result I was able to sing well throughout a Eucharist or a lengthy choir practice. I also found myself singing with deeper attention to the text, so that my singing became prayer.

On 1 September 2004, I had played for the observance of the Feast of Dedication of the Botham Road chapel. This was the last Eucharist celebrated there, and it was followed at once by the area bishop's reading the notice of deconsecration. I felt the bitter reality of something I loved coming to an end. I had played that organ for the better part of fifty years, and now it was to be dismantled, because the cost of rebuilding it would exceed the value of the instrument. The pipes would be stored and perhaps bought by some organ builder for reuse. The rest of the instrument, considered by our organ-servicing people as not worth salvaging, would be demolished with the chapel itself.

Sometime later, Sister Constance Joanna decided to advertise the organ, offering it gratis to anyone who would pay storage on the pipes and haul the rest away. Several people were interested, and the organ went to St. James' Church, Sharon, Ontario, for use in the new church they were about to build. So this lovely instrument, built in 1916 as a tribute to our Mother Foundress on her retirement, would be heard again—and perhaps I might have an opportunity to play it. To me it seemed like more than a reprieve from execution; it held the promise of a joyful resurrection. As if that were not enough, an anonymous donor undertook to pay the cost of building a tracker organ for our chapel. Even as I am writing this, an expert team of organ builders is installing this magnificent instrument into our chapel.

Opportunities came for me to share my experience of resurrection with others. When a woman staying in our Guest

House told me she had almost decided to give up playing the piano because of arthritis in her hands, I told her about our Sister Veronica, who had taught piano to children when she was in her eighties, saying that it was possible only because she kept playing the piano with her arthritic fingers. Then I told her my own story of having almost given up playing the organ. I said, "I know that I'll be able to do less and less as my Parkinson's progresses; but whatever stage I'm in, I'm determined to give it my best shot." I learned later that our conversation had restored her confidence and given her the encouragement she needed to keep on playing the piano.

Care partners or friends of people with Parkinson's, and the occasional person with Parkinson's, have talked with me during their stay in our Guest House. Sometimes I have been able to make concrete suggestions. Most of the time, however, people just want to talk with someone who knows from experience what they are going through. More than anything else, they value the assurance that they will be prayed for.

Sometime later, I had a still more dramatic resurrection. I had met Nancy Johnston, an associate professor in nursing at York University. She told me that she was writing a paper, "Finding Meaning in Adversity," that dealt with material similar to my own. So we exchanged manuscripts. As I read her essay, it dawned on me that I had experienced adversity at the depth she depicts it, many years before my diagnosis with Parkinson's. At the time, I sustained a wound that had never healed, took the bloom off my achievements, and filled me with self-doubt and, at times, self-hatred.

This was the shame, the sense of worthlessness and failure that I experienced when I abandoned my graduate studies and returned to the parental home and to jobs that anyone with a high school diploma could do. I can see now that I had counted so much on success as a scholar to prove my worth that, when I gave up my academic pursuits, I had nothing left to validate me and obtain the approval for which I was so needy. Sarcastic remarks, including those of a friend, about my being the "most highly educated secretary in Regina," reinforced my sense of failure. This, over the years, brought an ever-present dampening of delight in my achievements, a deep-seated conviction of my inadequacy, which undermined my successes.

As I read Nancy's essay and her quotations from people she had interviewed, it was as though a warm light was penetrating into the darkest corners, healing my self-hatred, filling me with joy and peace, and the knowledge that God's love for me was the foundation on which my life rested. Even the knowledge that at my age death could come at any time no longer terrified me. For me, it was more than a "taste" of resurrection; it was a banquet. No doubt I will be on short rations again, but I will with grace, be able to accept it as part of the normal ebb and flow of the spiritual life.

I felt ready to commit myself anew to the calling that brought me to SSJD in the first place—the Benedictine conviction that the bedrock of the monastic vocation is to "seek God." Even though God is the One in whom we live and move and have our being, we can through fear, busyness, or plain inertia put a "safe" distance between ourselves and the divine Lover. The contemplative way which monastic life offers is a simple, focused life lived for God, in God, and by the grace of God.

It is a challenging grace, an invitation to take responsibility for my life and relationship with my Redeemer. It is rather like leaving a teacher who goes by the book for another whose mission is to train students to think for themselves. Indeed, it is another transition—one that St. Paul described as a movement away from the law and toward the life in Christ.

I recognize that I have a long way to go. Old patterns die hard, and the strength of addiction is formidable. More often than not, I ignore the proffered grace of prayer and blithely launch into some project of my own. I find myself in the same place as St. Paul, who writes "I can will what is right, but I cannot do it. For I do not do the good I want, but the evil I do not want is what I do" (Romans 7:18-19). Paul sees this as delighting in the law of God, but subject to another law, making him captive to the law of sin.

When I call myself a sinner, I am not suggesting that the punding and workaholism are sinful in themselves. In the first place, the punding, at least, is a side-effect of my medication. The workaholism has been around for a long time, but I never thought of it as an addiction until now. What is new to me is the realization that they are models of the spiritual struggle described by Paul. Indeed, both are models of the fundamental sin of pitting my own will against that of God, which has hardened into a pattern of behaviour that I can scarcely control. Nevertheless, they offer the opportunity to rely on the grace of Christ, and to move beyond the lure of punding toward the goal of freedom in Christ.

This freedom is a gift, but it is a gift that challenges our will and our capacity for perseverance. It requires us to look at the actual circumstances of our day. When am I the most likely to pund? Clearly, when I get up in the morning. What do I really want and need first thing in the morning? Time for prayer. So I walk right over to my prayer corner and pray. Then I wash and dress, having decided the night before what I will be wearing and having put the clothes out to save time in the morning, and head off any lurking wish to pund. If time permits, I exercise. By this point my breakfast tray arrives. It is best for me to work on one problematic time and activity, and not move on until the new pattern is well established.

The difference between my lifelong self-preoccupation and the freedom we have in Christ was brought home to me when, just before evening prayer, Sister Brenda came over to me and asked me not to play so loud. I took offence, but managed not to show it. Inwardly, I was debating whether to play louder than ever or to play so softly as to be inaudible. Instead, I decided to adjust the volume so that it would be quieter but loud enough to give the singers the necessary support. As soon as I made this decision, the dark cloud that enveloped me lifted, the sun came out, the air was fresh, and I was smiling and at peace. I knew at once that this was the work of grace. I had been given the freedom to choose between the old response of anger and resentment and the new gift of humility and objectivity. By the end of the service I was taking pleasure not only in the part-singing, but in my role as accompanist, a contributor to the musical offering of praise and thanksgiving of the whole community. Before the day was over, I found an opportunity to thank Brenda for her intervention and all that flowed from it.

These personal experiences of resurrection here and now provide an answer to Nicodemus's question, "How can anyone be born after having grown old?" (John 3:4). These are gifts and insights that will take me the rest of my life to integrate fully, and I know that from time to time I will fall back into old ways. It behooves me to remember that I am dust. Recognition of finiteness, of mortality, must temper action and ground me in reality—all the more so since there are so few years between me and the fourscore that the psalmist considered a bonus. And what a life it has been! I give thanks for every moment of it. It seems to me that the rebirth of faith is retroactive in its effects, so that even my darkest moments have been illuminated by resurrection light.

No wonder, if I were asked to express in a single word what these four years since my diagnosis have meant to me, that word would be *grace*. Michael J. Fox has called Parkinson's "the gift that just keeps on taking" (*Lucky Man: A Memoir*. New York: Harper, 2002, p. 5), and this is true. But I have found again and again that what has been lost on one level is restored on another. And lost again. The gifts give me hope that lost ground can be recovered, if only temporarily. Nevertheless, the time comes to relinquish freely and generously, into the wounded hands of the Saviour, the gifts and the strengths we were entrusted with. As Teilhard de Chardin reminds us, eventually we will be overcome; but in the meantime, the forces of diminishment can become for us the appointed way of walking with our crucified and risen Saviour.

The gift that keeps on taking, yes—but a taking that bestows gifts that could not have come to me in any other way.

Suggestions for Reflection/Discussion

For Individuals

- What gifts have I received through the progress of my illness or aging process that I could not have had previously?

- Have I had "tastes of resurrection"? If so, how can I describe them? If I can't describe them, what might be getting in the way?

- How have my faith and God's grace been shown to be with me on this journey of illness and/or aging?

For Care Partners and Families
- What gifts do we receive from being close to someone who is ill or showing strong signs of aging?

For Small Groups
- Do the losses we have experienced provide us with "tastes of resurrection"?

- What have we learned about the life of a religious and of a religious community through the pages of this book? What has been important to apply to our lives in the broader community? In our congregation?

Postscript

In the summer of 2003, I was on holiday in our cottage on Mary Lake, a few miles south of Huntsville. One morning I awoke early, opened my curtains, and saw the quiet beauty of sunrise, tinting sky and lake with deep rose and burgundy, contrasting with the steely grey-blue of the water and the still black contours of Rocky Island. I watched until the colours faded into full daylight.

Before I realized what was happening, the words of a hymn were forming in my mind. Most poems I have written have required hard work and revision. This one was a sheer gift. I wrote the hymn—rather, the hymn virtually wrote itself, with very little effort on my part. It was not a question of God "dictating" the text to me; rather, it bore witness of the way that God may at times open the springs of creativity deep within each one of us.

I now offer my hymn to any who have read my story, and in great thanksgiving to God, Source of all being, eternal Word and Holy Spirit, who has so richly blessed my life. Amen, Alleluia!

Source, guide, and goal of all that is,
from whom my being flows,
direct my ways, make sure my steps
along the path you chose;
so may my life an offering be
to you, most holy Trinity.

Give me the grace to live this day
in peace and mindfulness,
discern your good and perfect will
in joy and in distress;
so let desire grow strong in me
for wholeness in your Unity.

May all, in stranger, friend, and foe
discern your image clear;
let anger, fear, mistrust, give way
to love that casts out fear;
so shall our lives an icon be
of your divine Community.

(Suggested tune: *O Jesu*, number 449 in *Common Praise*)

Suggestions for Reflection/Discussion

For Individuals

- What have I taken from this book that is most important for me at this point?

- What have I learned about living this experience with God's grace?

- When will I read the book again?

For Care Partners and Families
- What have we taken from this book that is most important for us at this point?

- What have we learned about living this experience of caring with God's grace?

For Small Groups
- Spend time with the hymn in this section. Discuss the important phrases in it for each of you. How do those phrases inform, enrich your lives?

Some Down-to-Earth Suggestions

The suggestion was made that it would be helpful, both to persons with Parkinson's and to health professionals, for me to write a kind of postscript giving some practical tips about how I have coped with day-to-day living. At the risk of repeating what has been said often, and by myself as well, I will offer some thoughts on what has helped me and those with whom I have contact.

Words on a hasti-note I have say it all: "If you want to be free, take your time, go slowly. Do few things, but do them well. Simple joys are holy" (*The Celtic Prayer Book*). Sometimes I feel overwhelmed by the day's tasks, or the clutter in my room, or all the letters I haven't answered—the list seems endless, and my strength and mental focus are no longer equal to it indefinitely. Every so often I come across two of my recorders (the alto I have already stored in the music practice room). I haven't played on them for years. I'd like to see if I can still play them well enough to make the practising worthwhile—but I need to discern whether they are part of my past or my future.

I find it helpful, when deciding if I should keep or get rid of something, to ask myself, "Is this part of my past or my future?" What about sewing? It is certainly part of my past and my present, but since I sew everything by hand, it takes me a long time to alter a garment. So although I surf the "free room" (where clothes Sisters no longer need are put out for others to use) almost daily, I have to ask myself, "How much alteration does this garment need? Have I the time or the skill to do a good job? Do I really need this garment? What might I part with in its place?" And so forth.

I need to keep in check the urge to go on working beyond my strength, or to crowd too many activities into one day. I need to take my time, and not set up quotas for myself. I need to respect my body, its signs of fatigue, its aches and pains, the emergence of symptoms. Rest and walking are good for the body.

Don't worry about conventions that make life more difficult for you. I have adopted the UUU (Unconventional Use of Utensils) system and don't worry about what Emily Post may have written. You work out the details; I find a tablespoon a versatile and useful aid.

My neurologist finds it very useful that I type up a fairly detailed account of what has happened since my last visit, reporting changes, recurrence of earlier problems, and anything that might have arisen out of what happened after the previous visit. I also send her e-mail reports between appointments when there is something I consider important, for example, a fall or series of falls, an episode of choking, and the onset of new symptoms or the increase of ones that I have had for some time.

Join a support group and invite any friends with PD you may have to come with you. If there is no support group where you live, consider starting one. Your local Parkinson Society office personnel will help you to get started and plan programs.

Use your innate ingenuity to work out original solutions, and share them with others.

Above all, be gentle with yourself and those around you. It has taken me several years to find the right tempo for walking, and I still have to remind myself to slow down. Forcing oneself to hurry is bad for body and soul alike. The corollary of this is that we need to allow the time needed now (not that of our pre-Parkinson days) to perform the various tasks of daily living. Otherwise we build up needless frustration and anxiety.

I close with some words from a letter written to me by Sister Nora. One of our most senior Sisters and not in the best of health, she was able to share these words of encouragement with me: "Bit by bit some of the delights go, but Oh how thankful for those that remain, and for new and different delights that come in very small ways, but delights."

More Suggestions from Others' Experience

Certain "challenges" confront someone with Parkinson's and make it increasingly difficult to accomplish tasks that used to be so easy. We can name a few of these challenges and discuss ways in which some people have suggested tackling them. Remember, there are as many "variables" with Parkinson's symptoms as there are people with Parkinson's. Symptoms affect one's ability to move but can also be the cause of numerous non-motor problems (e.g., thinking, bowel, bladder, balance, mood, and sexual issues).

To minimize the **fatigue** that you may experience: Take your time, go slowly (as if that's an option!). Steward your time and energy; allow the time it takes now, not the time it used to take, to complete a task; pace yourself and plan activities (including dressing, eating, socializing, etc.) for times that your medication is most likely to be working.

How can you maintain **independence** and control over some aspects of your life? Others have suggested that you "thumb your nose at conventions"! Be creative in finding different ways to do things that make them possible. Determine what you can still do, what contributions you can make, and concentrate on that. Get rid of false modesty, and don't hesitate to ask for assistance when you truly need it. Let others know what is and is not required, and don't be afraid to ask people not to do everything for you. When visiting health professionals, ask your doctors and nurses to speak directly to you instead of addressing a family member.

How can you make your life as **enjoyable** as possible? Try to continue to be as socially active as you have always been. By taking your medications before going out, you will be better able to enjoy activities. Don't hesitate to do, as someone with long-standing PD does, and quietly ask the waiter to cut your meat in the kitchen of the restaurant so you can enjoy your dinner out. Perhaps social activities will need to be adapted or changed altogether. For instance, if you enjoy playing cards with friends, but tremor makes it difficult to hold your cards, a piece of two-by-four wood with a groove cut along the length will hold your cards very nicely. Try to overcome feelings of embarrassment when you are with others. Admit to having Parkinson's. People will respond to your own secure self-image. Remember, many people are uncomfortable with illness: your attitude can help them.

How can you maintain a **positive attitude** and avoid the depression that can affect people with Parkinson's? Perhaps joining a support group would provide a beneficial opportunity to share time and conversation with others who are also living with Parkinson's. Support groups can also be a wonderful source of current information and education. But don't make Parkinson's your only community.

Knowledge and **acceptance** give you power! Accept the diagnosis; don't dwell on the prognosis. Adjust to adjusting. Determine what you can still do, what contributions you can still make and concentrate on that. Don't be afraid to teach others about Parkinson's: give your own Parkinson's 101.

Someone once said, "I have Parkinson's: Parkinson's doesn't have me." You aren't fighting with a monster, so make friends with your constant companion. Use your ingenuity and intelligence to out-trick Parkinson's; play games with your symptoms to overcome them. Above all, keep your sense of humour!

Suggestions for Care Partners

- Plan time together for activities you both enjoy. Make an effort to go somewhere special; choose one or two "big" events annually (such as a hot-air balloon ride). Check important details ahead of time—locate the washrooms and easiest exit. You may be exhausted, but it will be a worthwhile undertaking.
- Hold on to a sense of who you are—make time for whatever you enjoy. Stay with something really important for you.
- Keep a list of the things you need help with, and a list of those who have offered help. Don't become a martyr. You will be better able to cope if you have some ongoing help in the home.
- Make use of facilities in the community, such as home care, meals-on-wheels, and transportation services.
- Find people you can talk to in confidence. Care-partner groups can offer support and understanding with others in similar circumstances. Share with individuals who are not as far along the road: your experience can help someone else. And you might meet some new friends.
- Go with your partner to medical and other appointments. This can be a great way to gain information, express your concerns, and discuss treatment suggestions. Never

hesitate to inform the doctor or nurse of new or changed symptoms or medication effects.

- Recognize that your partner's symptoms are real and the frequent changes throughout a day are part of the disease and medication effects.
- Ask your doctor for a consultation with an occupational therapist to look at your living arrangement. Occupational therapists are good at reviewing the present situation and anticipating future needs.

There are experts available to speak with you, and many excellent resources available for the asking through the Parkinson Society Canada. In Ontario, contact Sandie Jones or Sarah Roojee at sarah.roojee@parkinson.ca or sandie.jones@parkinson.ca or call 1-800-565-3000/416-227-9700. In other parts of Canada, please contact Barbara Snelgrove at barbara.snelgrove@parkinson.ca or call 1-800-565-3000.

Path Books
A LIGHT TO MY PATH

We hope that you have enjoyed reading this Path Book. For more information about Path Books, please visit our web site at **www.pathbooks.com**. If you have coments or suggestions about Path Books, please write us at publisher@pathbooks.com.

Healing Families: Courage and Faith in Challenging Times
by Diane Marshall
From thirty years of counselling families, Diane Marshall offers constructive approaches to help family members respond to challenges such as time stress, discrimination, addiction, parenting, breakup — and to gain self-respect, a sense of competence, and spiritual connection.
1-55126-432-3, paper, 128 pages, $16.95

Oceans of Grief and Healing Waters: A Story of Loss and Recovery *by Marian Jean Haggerty*
With courageous candour and strength, Marian Haggerty tells the story of her journey toward healing from grief, after the death of a loved one.
1-55126-396-3, paper, 112 pages, $16.95

Healing Through Prayer: Health Practitioners Tell the Story *by Larry Dossey, Herbert Benson, John Polkinghorne, and Others*
Foreword by Peter Downie
1-55126-229-0, paper, 168 pages, $18.95

Sacred Simplicities: Seeing the Miracles in Our Lives
by Lori Knutson
In these engaging, two-page stories, Lori Knutson shares her experience of the divine in the everyday, and helps us to see glimpses of God where we least expect them. Here is enrichment for breaks at home, times of travel, meditations with nature, or even illustrations in sermons.
1-55126-419-6, paper, 160 pages, $18.95

Finer than Gold, Sweeter than Honey: The Psalms for Our Living *by Herbert O'Driscoll*
The psalms are among the most sublime poetry in the world, offering us inexhaustible wells of meaning. With adept artistry, Herbert O'Driscoll dips into their sacred depths and draws up sparkling insights to refresh the soul.

The reader will find rewarding insights and suggestions for personal reflection, daily journalling, group discussion, or sermon preparation.
1-55126-449-8, paper, 309 pages, $26.95